Welcome

t brings me great pleasure to welcome you to volume 12 of *Airliner Classics* as we embark on yet another journey through the golden age of commercial aviation, brought to you by the team behind *Airliner World*.

As a child growing up in Birmingham, many carefree afternoons were spent with my father or my aunt down at Elmdon airport, as we still called it then. The British Airways Birmingham liveried Boeing 737-236s, looking resplendent in their iconic Landor colours, or the One-Elevens of BA or their Birmingham/Brymon European partner with their deafening Rolls-Royce Spey engines, blasting off to some exciting destination, were what sparked my life-long love affair with aviation.

So it brings me great pleasure to tell the story behind not only British Airways at Birmingham, but also its wider regional empire, from the flag carrier's formation following the merger of British European Airways (BEA) and BOAC in 1974, to the BA Connect days and its takeover by Flybe.

Sticking with the UK flag carrier, Bob O'Brien recounts the early days of the 'Queen of the Skies' and how BOAC tailored its already renowned onboard service to suit the mammoth new arrival.

While it may seem strange to refer to easyJet as a 'classic' airline, the London/Luton-based low-cost giant has now been around for an incredible 30 years. During this time, it has worn several colour schemes, all in the iconic Pantone 021C orange, of course, and with artwork by Rolando Ugolini. We look back at the carrier's past three decades of history.

Robert Veitch charts the first half-century of the Spanish flag carrier Iberia as it gears up to celebrate its 100th anniversary in 2027. Meanwhile, Thomas Haynes tells the fascinating story of Air Afrique, a bold experiment in multinational aviation.

For our airport fans, we take you to the seaside and on a ride through the turbulent commercial history of Blackpool Airport, once a thriving regional gateway.

I was also lucky enough to chat to Andreas Christodoulides, to reveal the story behind Cyprus's first privately owned carrier, Helios Airways, and found that there was much more to the airline than the tragic crash most people remember it for.

Plus, we have stories on LTU's Lockheed L-1011 TriStars, Aviation Traders ATL90 Accountant, KLM's farewell to Fokker, plus not one, but two picture spreads from Liverpool's Speke Airport and the story of the world's first widebodied twinjet, the Airbus A300, and its smaller sibling, the A310.

I hope you enjoy reading this latest volume as much as we enjoyed putting it together.

Lee Cross
Assistant Editor, *Airliner World*

BELOW: KEY-LEE CROSS

44

Contents

104

14

84

60

37

AIRLINER Classics

Original cover art commissioned by Key Publishing and created by Antonis Karidis

ISBN: 978 1 83632 190 3
Editor: Lee Cross
Senior editor, specials: Roger Mortimer
Email: roger.mortimer@keypublishing.com
Cover Design: Steve Donovan
Design: SJmagic DESIGN SERVICES, India
Advertising Sales Manager: Sam Clark
Email: sam.clark@keypublishing.com
Tel: 01780 755131
Advertising Production: Becky Antoniades
Email: Rebecca.antoniades@keypublishing.com

SUBSCRIPTION/MAIL ORDER
Key Publishing Ltd, PO Box 300, Stamford, Lincs, PE9 1NA
Tel: 01780 480404
Subscriptions email: subs@keypublishing.com
Mail Order email: orders@keypublishing.com
Website: www.keypublishing.com/shop

PUBLISHING
Group CEO: Adrian Cox
Publisher: Steve O'Hara

Published by
Key Publishing Ltd, PO Box 100, Stamford, Lincs, PE9 1XQ
Tel: 01780 755131
Website: www.keypublishing.com

PRINTING
Precision Colour Printing Ltd, Haldane, Halesfield 1, Telford, Shropshire. TF7 4QQ

DISTRIBUTION
Frontline Distribution Solutions Ltd, 2 Poultry Avenue, London, EC1A 9PU
Enquiries Line: 02074 294000.

News 1940s

Viking's return to Copenhagen

BRITISH EUROPEAN Airways (BEA) introduced its new Vickers Viking into service on September 1, 1946. The maiden flight was operated between Northolt and Copenhagen, following a successful trial flight from Northolt to Oslo on August 20.

The Viking had been developed by Vickers using their Wellington bomber as the basis for the new commercial airliner. The first example took to the skies from the manufacturer's test airfield at Wisley, Surrey, on June 22, 1945, flown by chief test pilot Joseph 'Mutt' Summers. The third airframe to be built was delivered to BOAC on April 20, 1946, before being transferred to the newly established BEA later that year, following its formation by the British government to focus on

short-haul European and domestic services. (Photo British Airways)

TWA's Connie goes transatlantic

THE FIRST Lockheed L-049 Constellation belonging to Trans World Airlines (TWA) touched down at Paris/Orly on February 6, 1946, after a 16-hour 21-minute flight from New York/La Guardia. The aircraft, NC86511 (c/n 2035), appropriately named *Star of Paris*, had routed via Gander, Newfoundland, and Shannon, Ireland. The crew consisted of Captains Harold F Blackburn, Jack Herman and John M Clader, navigator M Chrisman and flight engineers Art Ruhanen, Ray McBride and Jack Rouge. Purser Don Shiemwell and flight attendant Ruth Schmidt looked after the 36 passengers onboard. A route proving trial from Washington/National had taken place two days earlier, flown by sistership NC86505 (c/n 2026).

The airline's owner, aviator Howard Hughes, had played a major part in the design and performance of the Constellation, following a meeting with Lockheed executives in June 1939 at a hotel in Beverly Hills, California. TWA subsequently placed an $18m order, signing an agreement with the manufacturer that would mean Lockheed could not sell the Connie to any other transcontinental airline until TWA had received 35 examples. (Photo Lockheed Martin)

International launch for Loftleiðir

ICELANDIC CARRIER Loftleiðir inaugurated its first flight between Iceland and the US on August 25, 1948. The flight to New York/Idlewild was operated following the arrival of the carrier's second 46-seat Douglas DC-4 Skymaster, called *Geysir*. The first, *Hekla*, had been scheduled to be delivered in 1946, making Loftleiðir the first Icelandic carrier to operate the type. However, delays caused by the bankruptcy of the firm that was meant to outfit the Skymaster's cabin led to a delay in launching international services. Its first international service, flying from Reykjavík to Copenhagen, was launched on June 17, 1947, coinciding with Icelandic National Day.

Loftleiðir was created in March 1944 by Icelandic businessman Alfreð Elíasson and two other Icelandic pilots who had been conducting training in Canada. Its first flight took place the following month, and previously the carrier had focused on domestic services from its Reykjavík base.

Convairliner touches down in the UK

ON AUGUST 28, 1948, the first Consolidated Convairliner, otherwise known as the CV 240-5, touched down for the first time at London/Heathrow Airport. The aircraft, VH-TAQ (c/n 64), which had departed from San Diego, California, was being delivered to Melbourne and its new operator, Trans-Australia Airlines (TAA). On board was the airline's technical superintendent, John Watkins, who explained that TAA had ordered five examples and would put them to work on the airline's busiest routes between the capitals on the East Coast of Australia. It currently employs Douglas DC-4s on these routes.

Northwest Orient welcomes first Stratocruiser

NORTHWEST ORIENT Airlines welcomed its first Boeing Model 377 Stratocruiser in June 1949 after a two-year production delay. The aircraft, N74601 (c/n 15947), revolutionised the carrier's transpacific services with unrivalled comfort and faster journey times.

The airline, which was rebranded as Northwest Orient in 1947, ordered ten examples of what was currently the largest civilian airliner for $15m in 1947. The Stratocruiser offered seating in the pressurised cabin for 69 passengers on the main deck and 14 in a novel downstairs lounge. Four Pratt & Whitney R-4360 Wasp Major radial piston engines allowed for cruising speeds of up to 325mph.

Pan American had been the 377's launch customer, having ordered 20 of the type in November 1945, which was then the largest aircraft order in history, valued at $24.5m.

Dublin Airport opens for business

THE INAUGURAL flight departed the new Dublin/Collinstown Airport, marking the new facilities' official opening at 0900hrs on January 19, 1940. The maiden service across the Irish Sea to Liverpool was operated by an Aer Lingus Lockheed 14, departing Collinstown's grass strip. The service was initially operated daily. The Lockheed 14 was Aer Lingus's first all-metal aircraft, joining the fleet in 1939.

Development of the new civilian aerodrome commenced in 1937, following the launch of Irish flag carrier Aer Lingus in 1936, which had intially been operating from Casement Aerodrome at Baldonnel.

In August 1938, work began on the new terminal building, designed by French-born architect Desmond Fitzgerald, who led the team of architects who developed the curved building with its tiered floors, heavily influenced by the great ocean liners at the time. Plans for concrete runways are underway to accommodate larger aircraft, allowing the airfield to expand its routes.

News 1950s

Ghana Airways welcomes Bristol Britannia

GHANA AIRWAYS welcomed a Bristol Britannia 102 to its fleet, which is being wet-leased from partner BOAC. The aircraft, G-ANBN (c/n 12915), still wears the basic BOAC livery, with Ghana Airways titles. It replaced the Boeing 377 Stratocruiser that has been operating flights between Accra and London.

The airline commenced operations after receiving its first aircraft, a de Havilland DH.114 Heron, 9G-AAA (c/n 14133), on December 30, 1958. Ghana Airways was established in July of that year with a start-up capital of £400,000. The new entity is a joint venture between the Ghanaian government, with a 60% stake, and BOAC. It has taken over the operations of the former West African Airways Corporation.

A seven-year agreement between the airline and BOAC has been signed that will see BOAC staff seconded to Accra to train

locals to run and operate the airline. (Photo Key Collection)

KLM purchases stake in Air Ceylon

DUTCH FLAG carrier KLM purchased the 49% stake in Air Ceylon from Australian carrier Australian National Airways (ANA) in 1955. The move followed the commencement of jet services by BOAC between London and Colombo with its de Havilland Comet jets in 1953. Following the grounding of the Comet in 1954, Air Ceylon leased a pair of Lockheed 749A Constellations for its flights to London.

The state-owned flag carrier of Ceylon (now Sri Lanka) can trace its history back to 1947, when the government purchased three Douglas DC-3s. It commenced commercial flights on December 10, 1947, from Colombo/Ratmalana heading to Madras via Palaly. The maiden flight, with 16 passengers onboard, was operated by DC-3, VP-CAR (c/n 25475) *Sita Devi*, with Captain Peter Fernando at the controls.

Air Ceylon had commenced flights to London using a pair of Douglas DC-4s, which had been leased from ANA after it had purchased a 49% stake in the start-up. Flights to Sydney, operated in co-operation with ANA, commenced in July 1950, routing via Singapore and Darwin.

BOAC's first 707 takes flight

THE FIRST Boeing 707-436 for BOAC took to the skies on May 19, 1959. The airframe, G-APFD (c/n 17705), is powered by four Rolls-Royce Conway engines, as opposed to the Pratt & Whitney JT3 powerplants typically found on the 707.

The move to use the Derby-built engines was part of the conditions set by the British government to allow the state-owned airline to order the US-built jet. The government had previously held a dim view of its airlines ordering foreign-built airframes and had wanted BOAC to stick with the upgraded Comet 4, of which it had ordered 19 examples in March 1955. BOAC was finally allowed to order 15 of the larger 707-400s, of which it was the launch customer, on November 15, 1956.

The UK Airworthiness Registration Board (ARB) has raised concerns about the 707's handling, which could necessitate modifications and subsequently delay type certification in the UK, ultimately impacting the type's entry into service.

Ireland goes transatlantic

ON APRIL 28, 1958, Aerlínte Éireann became the 17th airline to commence scheduled services across the Atlantic when operated a flight from Dublin to New York via Shannon. On board the Lockheed L-1049 Super Constellation were 99 passengers and six crew.

Before departure, a celebratory banquet was held, attended by then Taoiseach Éamon de Valera and Minister for Industry and Commerce Seán Lemass, the mayors of Dublin and New York, and a large press contingent. Upon arrival in the Big Apple, the aircraft was welcomed with a salute from the 165th Infantry of the New York National Guard.

The initial flight was operated by a Super Connie, N10009C, leased from Seaboard and Western Airlines. The airline has dubbed the type 'The Great Emerald Fleet'. In the cockpit were Seaboard and Western flight crew consisting of Captain Bill Donahue, assisted by relief Captain Joe O'Dwyer, first officer Bob McAllister, flight engineers Bob O'Donnell and Danny Been, plus navigator Mike Green. The operating crew were all Irish-Americans.

Sud Aviation Caravelle enters service with Air France

FRENCH FLAG carrier Air France has placed the Sud Aviation Caravelle into service. The inaugural flight from Paris/Orly departed for Rome/Ciampino on May 6, 1959, before continuing to Athens, with a final destination of Istanbul. The new jetliner replaced the airline's Lockheed Constellations that had previously flown the route.

Air France initially ordered 12 Caravelles on November 16, 1955, with options for an additional 12. It configured the aircraft with 20 seats in first class in a 2-2 layout and 55 in economy in a 2-3 layout.

The airline's next plan is to introduce the jet airliner on its lucrative Paris-London-Nice-London-Paris route. Sud Aviation rolled out the prototype Caravelle, F-WHHH (c/n 01), at Toulouse/Blagnac on April 21, 1955 and it then flew its maiden flight five weeks later, on May 27. Type certification was received on May 23, 1956.

However, authorities required that the Caravelle operate 1,500 hours of route-proving before it could enter service. Therefore, 'Hotel Hotel' was repainted in Air France colours and operated demonstration flights to potential customers. (Photo Key Collection)

News 1960s

Take off for One-Eleven

THE PROTOTYPE British Aircraft Corporation (BAC) One-Eleven has taken to the skies for the first time. The jet, G-ASHG (c/n BAC.004), took off from the firm's Hurn facility in Dorset on August 20, 1963, piloted by BAC's chief test pilot, Gabe 'Jock' Bryce, with Mike Lithgow, the One-Eleven's project pilot, operating as co-pilot. The inaugural flight comes well ahead of the One-Eleven's US-built rival, the Douglas DC-9, marking a massive coup for the British aviation industry.

'Hotel Golf' had rolled off the production line on July 28. At this point, the manufacturer had received orders from several carriers, including Braniff International and Mohawk Airlines in the US.

The One-Eleven was conceived by Hunting Aircraft as the H.107, a 30-seat jet airliner, in the 1950s. Following the merger of several other aircraft manufacturers to form BAC, the aircraft was stretched to 79 seats and designed as a short-range jet. It was publicly launched on May 9, 1961, following an order for ten Series 200s

by UK independent carrier British United Airways.

After more flights from Hurn, the prototype will be flown to the company's test airfield at Wisley in Surrey, where flight testing will begin in earnest. (Photo BAE Systems)

Royal opening for East Midlands Airport

THE NEW East Midlands Airport was officially opened by HRH The Duke of Edinburgh on July 2, 1965. The redevelopment of the former RAF Castle Donington took 13 months to complete and cost approximately £1.4m.

East Midlands Airport was first conceived in 1963, when the county and city councils of Derbyshire, Derby, Leicestershire, Leicester, Nottinghamshire and Nottingham purchased the former RAF base to redevelop the site as a civilian airfield, replacing Burnaston, which only had a grass runway.

The first flight from Glasgow touched down on April 2, 1965, operated by local carrier Derby Airways, which had relocated its operation from Burnaston.

Braniff heads to Honolulu

BRANIFF INTERNATIONAL commenced nonstop flights from Dallas/Love Field to Honolulu, Hawaii, on August 14, 1969. The inaugural sold-out flight, BN501, was flown by one of the carrier's Boeing 707-327Cs wearing Braniff's iconic 'The End of the Plain Plane' livery and was packed full of Braniff's senior management.

Captain M.W. 'Mal' Sellmeyer was at the controls, and he and his colleagues were handed a traditional Hawaiian lei by Hawaiian Airlines officials before departure. Upon arrival, the aircraft was greeted by Hawaiian dignitaries and the reigning Miss Hawaii, who welcomed the reigning Miss Texas, who had also been on the flight.

The airline's vice president of regulatory proceedings, Tom Robertson, had applied for the transpacific route on February 23, 1966, and it was subsequently approved on January 4, 1969.

The airline plans to add additional services to the Pacific island from Atlanta and Houston in September, as well as increasing the frequency of the Dallas rotation to twice daily.

BOAC places Super VC10 into service

THE FIRST Vickers Super VC10 for BOAC has entered service between London/Heathrow and New York/JFK, before continuing on to San Francisco. The maiden service, operated by G-ASGD (c/n 854), took off on April 1, 1965, on the airline's 'Monarch' service, which also serves Bermuda and San Francisco. In command of the flight was Captain Norman Todd.

Ten of the 'Super' variant, which had a 4.6m stretch over the standard model, had been ordered in June 1960 at a cost of £25m. However, BOAC had wanted to order more of the VC10's US rival, the Boeing 707.

BOAC already uses the 139-seat Standard VC10. The first example, G-ARVI (c/n 811), entered service with the airline on April 19, 1964, from Heathrow to Lagos. It had ordered 35 of the standard variant in January 1958, with options for a further 20 for use on the carrier's 'Empire' routes. This

was the minimum number Vickers required to break even on the VC10, allowing the manufacturer to proceed with the jet's development. This order subsequently changed in 1961 to 12 standard and 30 Rolls-Royce Conway Mk. 301 turbofan-powered 'Super' VC10s, although it seems likely that this order will also change to meet the airline's requirements, as the Super VC10 does not match the performance of the 707.

Trident heads to Kuwait

The maiden Hawker Siddeley HS-121 Trident 1E for Kuwait Airways took to the skies for the first time on March 5, 1966. The aircraft, currently registered G-ASWU (c/n 2114), will be re-registered as 9K-ACF upon delivery at the end of March.

The trijet was originally built as a Trident 1C for British European Airways, but has been converted to the improved 1E variant. Kuwait Airways first placed an order with the British manufacturer on August 8, 1962, signing a deal for two jets, with options on a third.

The Trident 1E is an upgraded version of the Trident 1C. To improve the jet's airfield performance, Hawker Siddeley has increased the size of the wing and flap span, and also replaced the drooped leading edge with leading-edge slats. It offers increased fuel capacity and all-round higher operating weights and payload than its predecessor. This, in part, is also thanks to the jet's upgraded 11,400lb Spey 511 engines. Despite having the same fuselage length as the 1C, the Trident 1E accommodates more passengers thanks to a redesigned cabin. (Photo Key Collection)

News 1970s

Paris/Charles de Gaulle ouvrir!

THE BRAND-NEW airport to serve the French capital, Paris/Charles de Gaulle, officially opened on March 8, 1974. It is now home to the country's flag carrier, Air France, and Union de Transports Aériens (UTA).

Plans for Charles de Gaulle, to be known as Aéroport de Paris Nord (Paris North), date back to 1957, when

the country's government decided a new facility was required to relieve pressure on Paris/Orly. A site was chosen 25km north of the city and the final master plan for the airport was produced by several designers, led by chief engineer Jacques Block.

Construction began in December 1966 and, after eight years and a cost of $275m, the airport was completed. It is named after the French President who led the Free French Forces during World War Two, before establishing the French Fifth Republic.

Architect Paul Andreu designed Terminal 1. Its iconic circular design features a central ten-storey core and seven adjoining satellites, accessed via under-apron walkways. At apron level, there is sufficient space for aircraft to taxi between the structures, and the gates are located in the remote buildings. A further circular taxiway surrounds the entire terminal, enabling aircraft to circulate around it in both directions.

The main structure is not completely solid, as it appears from afar, but is actually a ring, open at its centre. It is criss-crossed by several glass-clad moving walkways that convey travellers between floors. The lower levels include shops, bus and service vehicle access points, while check-in and baggage reclaim take place on a floor slightly higher than the apron level. There are offices, airline lounges and car parks on the upper levels. (Photo Air France)

Dan-Air buys Skyways International

DAN-AIR HAS acquired Ashford-based Skyways International. The deal, for £650,000, was signed in February 1972, following the decision by Skyways owners, Sterling Industrial Securities, to offload the troubled airline. As part of the agreement, Dan-Air will inherit four of the airline's Hawker Siddeley HS 748s. Dan-Air has said that it will integrate the majority of Skyways'

routes into its own network, which will initially be operated as a subsidiary known as Dan-Air Skyways.

Skyways International was established in February 1971, following the liquidation of the former Skyways Coach-Air on January 20, 1971. The latter had previously survived the sale of its Skyways Group stablemate, Skyways Limited, to Euravia in 1962.

On September 30, 1955, the airline launched the world's first low-fare scheduled service between London and Paris, utilising a Douglas DC-3 that flew from Lympne, Kent to Paris/Beauvais.

This subsequently led to the creation of Skyways Coach-Air in 1958 as a dedicated low-fare subsidiary of the Skyways Group.

British Aerospace is born

THE UK has a new aircraft manufacturer, British Aerospace (BAe), with its head office located at the former British Aircraft Corporation (BAC) site in Weybridge.

The new state-owned company came into being on April 29, 1977, following the introduction of the Aircraft and Shipbuilding Industries Act, which saw the merger of BAC, Hawker Siddeley Aviation, Hawker Siddeley Dynamics and Scottish Aviation. The aim is to streamline the UK's aerospace capabilities and enhance competitiveness.

The merger makes BAe one of the world's largest aerospace companies, employing approximately 76,000 people in the UK and overseas. It offers a range of products that is currently unmatched by any other aerospace firm. BAe has also inherited several aircraft programmes from its predecessors, namely Scottish Aviation's Jetstream and the Hawker Siddeley HS 125 business jet. Production of the HS 748 turboprop, as well as the BAC One-Eleven and BAC/Aérospatiale Concorde, will also continue.

BA receives first TriStar

British Airways has received its first Lockheed L-1011 TriStar 1. The aircraft, G-BBAE (c/n 193N-1083) *The Stargazer Rose*, was delivered to the airline's London/Heathrow base on October 21, 1974, looking resplendent in the carrier's new Negus & Negus designed livery. The following day, it flew to Berlin to represent the airline at the official opening of the City's Tegel airport.

The airline plans to put the type into service in early 1975. They are configured with 320 seats, 20 in first class and 300 in economy.

British Airways inherited the TriStar order from British European Airways (BEA), which had first signed up for the jet on August 7, 1972, initially agreeimg a deal for six TriStar 1s, with options on six more. (Photo Key Collection)

American Airlines places the DC-10 into service

AMERICAN AIRLINES has placed its first McDonnell Douglas DC-10 into commercial service. The maiden flight, on August 5, 1971, was operated by DC-10-10, N103AA (c/n 46503), between Los Angeles and Chicago/O'Hare.

Dubbed by the airline as the 'Luxury Liner', American was the

joint launch customer with United Airlines, after initially ordering 25 examples with options for a further 25 on February 19, 1968.

The aircraft was designed as a widebody replacement for the Douglas DC-8 and first flew on August 29, 1970. American had approached the manufacturer to

create a twin-aisle jet, smaller than the Boeing 747 but with long-range capabilities and the performance to operate from airports with shorter runways. It is the first aircraft to be produced under the McDonnell Douglas name after the merger of Douglas and the McDonnell Aircraft Corporation in 1967.

News 1980s

First 747-400 for British Airways

BOEING HELD a special ceremony in Seattle to mark the handover of the first two 747-436s destined for British Airways (BA). The event, which took place on June 30, 1989, was attended by BA chairman Lord King of Wartnaby. The first two Rolls-Royce RB211-powered jets destined for the airline are G-BNLA (c/n 23908) *City of London* and G-BNLC (c/n 23910) *City of Cardiff*. The type is expected to enter service with BA between London/Heathrow and Philadelphia on July 27, 1989.

The UK flag carrier first ordered 16 of the latest member of the 747 family on August 16, 1986, with options on a further 12. The deal was the highest-value aircraft order ever placed, with each airframe costing $4.3m.

The Boeing 747 has played an important role in the BA fleet since the arrival of its first -136 variant, G-AWNF (c/n 19766), on April 14, 1971, with the airline's predecessor, BOAC. BA also operates the 747-236,

the final examples of which were delivered in 1988. (Photo British Airways Heritage Collection)

Air UK Leisure becomes Europe's first 737-400 operator

LONDON/STANSTED-BASED CHARTER carrier AirUK Leisure has become Europe's first operator of the Boeing 737-400. The airline welcomed its first example, G-UKLA (c/n 23865), on October 14, 1988.

AirUK Leisure, a joint venture between AirUK and travel group Viking International, was first announced in June 1987. The former provided 30% of the £2.5m capital, while the rest came from Viking. Operations commenced with a pair of Boeing 737-200s: G-BMOR (c/n 21775) and G-BNZT (c/n 22703), which flew from London Stansted to Faro.

Ansett receives first 767

AUSTRALIAN CARRIER Ansett Airlines has become the country's first operator of the Boeing 767, after receiving its first 767-277, VH-RMD (c/n 22692). The aircraft touched down at the company's Sydney/Kingsford Smith base on June 10, 1983, after a transpacific delivery flight.

As the airline's first widebodied jets, Ansett's 767s have been built with a three-man flight deck, to include a flight engineer's position. This came following demands from the pilot and flight engineer unions, who insisted that the flight engineers' role be retained, despite the aircraft being designed for a two-person operation. Boeing accommodated the airline's request by building the first 30 aircraft with the necessary flight engineer stations.

Ansett ordered five 767-200s in March 1980 as part of a 21-aircraft deal with the US manufacturer at a cost of around $600m. Alongside the 767s, the order also included 12 737-200s and four 727-200LRs. (Photo Boeing)

Flights begin at London/City

PASSENGER SERVICES have commenced at London/City Airport. The maiden flight to Plymouth took off on October 26, 1987, and was flown by one of the facility's biggest supporters, Brymon Airways.

To create the airport, land has been reclaimed from King George V Dock in London's Docklands. Currently, the airport has a single runway, measuring 1,080m, and a terminal building designed by R Seifert and Partners to resemble a dockside warehouse. On the apron, there are four aircraft parking stands.

The idea for an airport in Docklands was first put forward in 1981 by the London Docklands Development Corporation. A year later, Brymon Airways made history by landing one of its Pratt & Whitney Canada PT6A-50-powered De Havilland Dash 7 turboprops on a makeshift runway at Heron's Quay. The flight, which took place on June 27, 1982, was flown by Brymon's chief pilot, Harry Gee, and demonstrated the type's ability to operate safely from a short landing strip in a built-up area.

The airline then submitted route licence applications to the Civil Aviation Authority (CAA) for services to Aberdeen, Belfast, Birmingham, the Channel Islands, East Midlands, Manchester, Paris and Rotterdam. On May 31, 1987, Dash 7 G-BRYB (c/n 66), appropriately named *City of London*, was the first aircraft to land at the new facility.

In addition to Brymon, London/City is also served by London City Airways, which was established by British Midland Airways with a fleet of Dash 7s.

AirCal flies into the sunset

AIRCAL HAS been officially merged into its new owner, American Airlines, with the name and colourful livery disappearing on July 1, 1987. Its fleet of Boeing 737s and BAe 146s will be transferred to American, along with many of its employees.

The airline had accepted a $225m offer from American Airlines on November 17, 1986. Speaking at the time, AA's chairman and CEO Robert L Crandall said: "The AirCal acquisition will allow American to fulfil its plans to develop its new hubs at Nashville, Raleigh-Durham and San Juan, while simultaneously developing a substantial West Coast operation."

Based at Orange County Airport, AirCal began operations as Air California in 1967, initially flying as an interstate airline with a pair of former American Airlines Lockheed L-188 'Prop-Jet' Electras. Its maiden route between Orange County and San Francisco was served up to five times per day. Further Electras were added before the arrival of its first jets, the Douglas DC-9-14, in 1968. However, these were a stopgap until it received its first Boeing 737-200s in July that year.

In 1981, Air California was acquired by the Westgate Corporation in a deal valued at $61.5m. It was then rebranded to AirCal with a striking new livery, designed to portray the warmth and colours of a California sunrise.

Despite the merger, AirCal did manage to celebrate its 20th anniversary on January 16, before the takeover was completed and approved by the Transportation Department on March 30.

Special colours for Concorde

TO MARK the 20th anniversary of Concorde's maiden flight, one of the first production aircraft, F-WTSB (c/n 100-001), has been painted in a special livery designed by Czech artist Pavel Smetana and painted by students from the Paris School of Arts. The eyecatching look, featuring a glittering red, white and blue, was unveiled at a special anniversary event held in Toulouse in March 1989.

News 1990s

MD-90 takes to the skies

THE PROTOTYPE McDonnell Douglas MD-90 has taken to the skies for its first flight. The maiden sortie saw the jet depart from the manufacturer's Long Beach, California, site on February 22, 1993.

The development of the largest member of the Douglas DC-9/McDonnell Douglas MD-80 family, the -90, began in the early 1980s. The jet is powered by two International Aero Engines (IAE) V2500 turbofan engines. The manufacturer had previously looked at powering its newest model with two propfan engines, but delays and mounting costs led to the termination of this project.

The MD-90 features an advanced flight deck with an electronic flight instrument system (EFIS), a full flight management system, a state-of-the-art inertial reference system and LED dot-matrix displays for engine and system monitoring.

Delta Air Lines is the launch customer of the MD-90. It placed an order for 50 examples on November 14, 1989, with options for a further 110. The Atlanta-based carrier intends to use the type to replace its Boeing 727 fleet. (Photo Key Collection)

Adiós Aviaco

AVIACIÓN Y Comercio, better known as Aviaco, operated its final flight on September 1, 1999, after being absorbed into its parent, Iberia. The Spanish flag carrier had purchased all the remaining shares of Aviaco in 1998, adding its 'IB' IATA code to all the carrier's flights. At the time, Iberia also announced an order for 76 Airbus A320s, aimed at streamlining its short-haul operations.

Aviaco can trace its history back to 1948, when it was established by the National Institute of Industry to supplement Iberia's regional network, which was limited at the time. Operations began in September that year with a fleet of three Bristol 170s, flying between Madrid, Bilbao and Barcelona. During the 1960s, the airline experienced significant growth and the Spanish government decided to establish a joint board for Aviaco and Iberia to better co-ordinate the operations of both carriers.

Charter operations grew, and in the 1980s, the carrier's Douglas DC-9 jets were frequently seen at airports across Europe. It also continued to develop a profitable regional network, which, despite accounting for only 30% of its flights, generated 70% of its revenue.

Finnair places MD-11 into service

AFTER RECEIVING its first MD-11 airframe, OH-LGA (c/n 48449), on December 7, 1990, Finnair has placed the type into service, flying from Helsinki to Tenerife on December 20.

The carrier was the launch customer for the McDonnell Douglas trijet, after placing an order for four examples. Finnair intended to use them to replace its ageing DC-10 fleet and expand its growing Europe-Asia network, after becoming the first Western airline to fly nonstop between Europe and China in 1988.

McDonnell Douglas launched the MD-11 programme on December 30, 1986, after the Long Beach manufacturer received firm orders for 52 airframes, plus 40 options on three variants: passenger, combi and freighter. Finnair was one of nine other airlines that signed up for the jet, including Alitalia, British Caledonian, Dragonair, Korean Air, SAS Scandinavian Airlines, Swissair, Thai Airways International and Varig.

Canada 3000 welcomes first A330-200

Canada 3000 became the launch customer of the Airbus A330-200, after receiving its first example, C-GGWA (c/n 205), on May 29, 1998. The aircraft is configured in a 340-seat all-economy layout, and will be put into service initially between Toronto and Vancouver for crew training before being deployed on transatlantic services.

The Toronto-based charter carrier had been evaluating several long-haul types from both Airbus and Boeing to complement its Boeing 757 fleet, which it uses on inclusive tour flights to the Caribbean, Europe, Florida and Hawaii. It subsequently signed a lease deal with ILFC for up to four A330-200s in September 1996, becoming the North American launch customer of the A330. The airline selected General Electric's CF6-80E1 engine to power the fleet.

The prototype A330-200, F-WWCB (c/n 871), first flew on August 13, 1997, from Toulouse/Blagnac Airport. This was followed by a 16-month, 630-hour test flight programme before it was certified.

Take-off for A321

THE NEWEST member of the Airbus A320 Family, the stretched A321, has completed a successful maiden flight.

The aircraft, wearing test registration F-WWIA (c/n 364), took off from the planemaker's Hamburg/Finkenwerder plant on March 11, 1993, under the command of test pilot Karl-Eugen Nagel.

The maiden sortie lasted four hours and 37 minutes. During this time, the International Aero Engine (IAE) V2500-powered aircraft cruised over northern Germany and the North Sea, while nine tonnes of test equipment carried aboard monitored its performance.

A second prototype, powered by CFM International CFM56-5B engines, is due to enter the test programme shortly.

Airbus launched the stretched A321 on November 24, 1988, following the entry into service of its smaller sibling, the A320, with Air France. It is 6.94m longer than the A320, with the capacity to carry up to 224 passengers in a single-class configuration.

The German flag carrier, Lufthansa and the Italian flag carrier, Alitalia were the type's joint launch customers, having placed orders for 20 and 40 examples, respectively. (Photo Airbus)

News 2000s

Delta and United retire trijets

DELTA AIR Lines and United Airlines have retired their last trijet aircraft from their fleets.

The first to make the move was Delta, with its Lockheed L-1011 TriStars. The final service, DL1949, was flown on July 31, 2001, between Orlando and Atlanta. The L-1011-1, N728DA (c/n 1178), was under the command of Captain Randell Schmoyer. The aircraft entered service with the airline on February 18, 1980. The Atlanta-based carrier received its first 'ten eleven', N701DA (c/n 1041), on October 3, 1973. Over the years, Delta flew a total of 70 TriStars, more than any other airline in the world. At its peak in the 1990s, it had 56 in its fleet.

Meanwhile, United retired its last McDonnell Douglas DC-10 after 30 years of service. The final flight was operated in two segments on February 14, 2001. Flight UA700 between Las Vegas and Chicago was operated by DC-10-30 N1858U (c/n 46987), an ex-World Airways example, which was delivered to United in May 1986. Meanwhile, N1857U (c/n 46986), also a former World Airways series -30, operated flight UA44 between Honolulu and Chicago.

Captain Tom Harvey, assisted by first officer NC Garthus and second officer LC Paulin, was the crew of flight 700, and the trijet was treated to a water cannon salute and farewell by many of the airline's ground staff as it departed Las Vegas.

United placed an order for 30 DC-10s on April 25, 1968, with options for

an additional 30 airframes. The first to be delivered on July 29, 1971, was N1802U (c/n 46601). It was placed into service between San Francisco and Washington/Dulles on August 14. Over the years, the airline has operated a total of 59 DC-10s, comprising both the -10 and -30 series. At its peak, United had 49 DC-10s in service. The final two examples were then delivered to their new owner, Finova Capital. (Photo Delta Air Lines)

First next-gen 737 for easyJet

LONDON/LUTON-BASED EASYJET has received its first next-generation Boeing 737-700. The aircraft, G-EZJA (c/n 30235), was delivered to the airline on October 15, 2000. According to Boeing, the low-cost carrier plans to operate more than 40 of the world's best-selling jetliners on 28 routes to 18 destinations within Europe by 2004.

"We have a high frequency operation that requires the near-perfect reliability of the 737, and the advantages of being an all-Boeing operation save us enormous time and money on maintenance, training and ground operations," said easyJet chairman Stelios Haji-Ioannou. "With this new member of the next-generation 737 family, our Europe route network becomes stronger and is able to grow."

With the addition of the -700 series, easyJet will operate one of the world's youngest fleets of 737s, with the average age being four years old.

"The 737 provides optimal solutions for easyJet for both its international

and domestic routes," said Toby Bright, Boeing Commercial Airplanes Group vice president - European sales. (Photo easyJet)

Cyprus Airways welcomes first A330

CYPRIOT FLAG carrier, Cyprus Airways, has continued its fleet modernisation programme and transition to an all-Airbus fleet, after receiving the first of two A330-200s, 5B-DBS (c/n 505) *Famagusta*, on lease from ILFC. The aircraft will be used to replace the airline's four ageing A310-200s, which have been deployed since 1984.

The Larnaca-based airline has configured its widebody jets with 30 seats in business class and 265 in economy class. They will be placed into service on the airline's flagship service between Larnaca and London/Heathrow in January 2003.

British Midland rebrands

THE UK'S second-largest airline, British Midland, has rebranded itself as bmi British Midland, with its official name being British Midland International. The airline unveiled the change on February 1, 2001. The name change coincides with the unveiling of a new livery of royal blue, white and a fading, stylised union flag design on the tail, created by Landor Associates. The rollout is expected to cost around £20m and is scheduled to be completed within the next 18-24 months.

Landor said that the redesign was the result of a "very strong collaboration" between the design firm and the airline. Everything from the corporate identity of the carrier down to the aircraft cabins, lounges and even the cocktail stirrers onboard will be rebranded. For the first time, passengers seated in bmi British Midland's new business class cabin will be treated to freshly prepared food served by an onboard chef.

Long-haul flights will also be relaunched for the first time in 18 years. After initially placing options on two Boeing 767-300ERs and two Airbus A330-200s, the airline eventually settled on the latter, signing a $1.2m deal for four airframes with options on eight more in February 2000. The first example, G-WWBM (c/n 398), touched down at Manchester on April 27, 2001, and will be used to operate transatlantic flights from its northwest hub to Washington DC and Chicago. The airline had hoped to fly from its London/Heathrow base, but it was unable to obtain the necessary traffic rights.

Air Astana takes to the skies

THE CENTRAL Asian Republic of Kazakhstan has a new airline after Air Astana operated its maiden flight from Almaty to Nur-Sultan on May 15, 2002. A special ceremony was held before the flight, attended by the first President of Kazakhstan, Nursultan Nazarbayev, and Sir Richard Evans from British Aerospace (BAe).

The airline was established in 2001 at the request of Nazarbayev, who sought to create a world-class carrier compliant with international standards. Together with the UK aerospace giant BAe, the republic's government invested $17m in the start-up. It aimed to operate as both a domestic and second-level carrier alongside Air Kazakhstan.

A month after commencing operations, Air Astana received its first Boeing 737-800, P4-BAS (c/n 30627), on lease from ILFC. It joined a pair of Boeing 737-700s – P4-CAS (c/n 30629) and P4-DAS (c/n 30642) – also on lease from ILFC.

A 300 B a Reality
AEROSPATIALE/FRANCE . DEUTSCHE AIRBUS (MBB and VFW) . HAWKER SIDDELEY . FOKKER
Airbus Industrie , 160 Avenue de Versailles , Paris 16ᵉ , France

Iberia's first 50

AS IBERIA HEADS TOWARDS IT'S 2027 CENTENARY, ROBERT VEITCH LOOKS BACK AT THE LIFE AND TIMES OF THE AIRLINE DURING ITS FIRST HALF-CENTURY

ABOVE: The last de Havilland DH.89 Dragon Rapide in Iberia service was EC-AAS (c/n 6424), which was retired in 1955 IBERIA

BELOW: Iberia McDonnell Douglas DC-10-30 EC-DEA (c/n 47982) *Rías Gallegas* was one of 13 of the type operated between 1973 and 2005 MCDONNELL-DOUGLAS VIA JOSÉ RAMÓN VALERO

beria was founded as Compañía Aérea de Transporte on June 28, 1927, financed with 836,000 pesetas (Pts) from its first president, Horacio Echevarrieta, and 264,000 Pts from Deutsche Luft Hansa (later to be rebranded as Lufthansa). The fleet comprised three former Luft Hansa Rohrbach Roland tri-motors costing 600,000 Pts, which flew at speeds of up to 127mph, had capacity for ten passengers and three crew, and boasted an onboard toilet.

The fledgling airline first took to the skies on December 14, on a flight inaugurated by King Alfonso XIII between Madrid/Cuatro Vientos and Barcelona, which took three-and-a-half hours. Tickets cost 163 Pts one-way or 300 Pts for a round trip, with 15kg of baggage included. There were two daily flights in each direction and 287 people used the service in the first month, with a load factor of 60%. To obtain a license, the pilot test involved flying 300km without an instructor, performing five figure-of-eights at an altitude of 200m and landing less than 100m from a signal – their main enemy was fog.

The following year, under Miguel Primo de Rivera's authoritarian government, the new airline was amalgamated with Ceta and Unión Aérea Espanola into the state-controlled Compañía de Líneas Aéreas Subvencionadas (CLASSA). On May 27, 1929, a Junkers G-24 departed Madrid/Getafe for Seville, becoming CLASSA's first scheduled flight. On August 19, it established a service between Madrid and Biarritz, which marked the beginning of international Spanish commercial aviation. Services to the Canary Islands were initiated on May 27, 1930, with a Ford 4-AT trimotor, the only aircraft in the fleet with an onboard radio, with stops in Casablanca and Cape Juby on the way to Las Palmas and, finally, Tenerife/Norte.

With the establishing of the Second Spanish Republic in 1931, CLASSA was replaced by Líneas

"In early 1935 the company decided to buy two Douglas DC-2s and legend has it that the contract was signed on a cigarette paper in Amsterdam"

ABOVE: Iberia's original fleet comprised a trio of Rorhbach Rolands, including M-CBBB (c/n 19) IBERIA

New York, New York

At 2100hrs on August 3, 1954, Flight 951 from Madrid/Barajas to New York/Idlewild commenced with Lockheed L-1049G Super Constellation EC-AIN (c/n 4550) *Santa Maria*. After 15 hours, and after enduring problematic weather en route, the invitation-only rotation touched down in the Big Apple.

The first scheduled flight in a thrice-weekly service followed on August 8, with 19 first class seats available at $436 each, while 55 economy seats were available for $334. During the first five months, 1,992 passengers flew the route, which increased to 7,300 across 1955.

By 1979, the route's 25th anniversary, more than 2.2 million passengers had made the nine-hour Atlantic crossing. To help penetrate a US market dominated by TWA and Pan Am, Iberia signed with advertising and public relations agency James Seix, whose initial advice was to change the name of the airline to Iberia, Líneas Aéreas de España.

Aéreas Postales Españolas (LAPE) and the new entity joined the Association of European Airlines trade body. In 1932, the Madrid-Casablanca-Las Palmas service was established and, in August 1934, the Valencia route commenced from the newly opened Madrid/Barajas. In early 1935, the company decided to buy two Douglas DC-2s and legend has it that the contract was signed on a cigarette paper in Amsterdam. After it became the first non-French airline to be granted rights to an internal route, the DC-2s were put to work operating from Paris to Bordeaux.

The 1940s

Between 1936 and 1939, during the Spanish Civil War, the airline continued to operate sporadically from temporary headquarters in Salamanca, reverting to the Iberia name. In August 16, 1937, the first Iberia route was inaugurated – Vitoria-Burgos-Salamanca-Cáceres-Seville-Tetuán – and, on September 21, the second was Santiago de Compostela-Valladolid-Salamanca. In 1939, after the Civil War ended, the airline was nationalised and a new Iberia livery was introduced. The headquarters returned to Madrid, the registration prefix changed from 'M' to 'EC' and new routes from Madrid to Valencia and Lisbon were introduced.

On October 4, 1940, another airline, Transporte Aéreos Españoles, was merged into Iberia, resulting in the creation of a new company called Compañía Mercantil Anónima Iberia. World War Two led to fuel and spare parts shortages and the airline suspended most routes, with the exception of Seville-Tétouan-Melilla and Santa Isabel-Bata. Only the twin-engine de Havilland DH.89 Dragon Rapides were able to operate, as they ran on standard automotive petrol. There was also some expansion with three Douglas DC-3s added to the fleet after inadvertently landing in the Spanish zone of the Moroccan protectorate. The Spanish government negotiated their acquisition with its US counterpart, later transferring them to Iberia.

On September 30, 1944, the airline was incorporated into the state-owned Instituto Nacional de Industria (INI). The purchase of seven DC-3s and three DC-4s was finalised to add to a fleet comprising four DC-2s, four De Havilland DH.89 Dragon Rapides and several Junkers aircraft. In 1945, it joined the newly formed International Air Transport Association (IATA). »

BELOW: The airline operated Junkers G-24s between 1929 and 1936 IBERIA

The first regular service between Europe and South America was inaugurated on September 22, 1946, when a Douglas DC-4, departed Madrid/Barajas. After stops in Villa Cisneros (Dakhla), Natal, Rio de Janeiro and Montevideo, it arrived at Buenos Aires/Morón 36 hours later to an enthusiastic reception. Onboard meals had included a plate of charcoal-grilled chicken with fried fish, Spanish omelette, hardboiled eggs and garlic. The route proved a success and, despite a ticket costing 7,250 Pts, flights operated at 90% capacity. By the end of the year, Iberia had flown 113,530 passengers – almost double the 1945 total – with a load factor of 87.5%, and carried 3,000 tonnes of cargo, all made possible with 27 aircraft, 57 flight crew and a staff of 800 people.

On February 18, 1948, an air transport company operating Bristol 170 freighters was established in Bilbao under the name Aviación y Comercio (Aviaco). It would take until September 19 for the first commercial flight to depart Bilbao's new airport for Madrid. A second weekly route followed on May 15, 1949: Madrid-Sal/Amílcar Cabral-Caracas-San Juan/Luis Muñoz Marín, returning via Bermuda and The Azores to Madrid. The following year, services to Mexico City and Havana began.

The 1950s

As 1950 rolled around, Iberia incorporated four more DC-4s into its fleet to enable the strengthening of existing services and launch new ones. It then purchased three Lockheed L-1049G Super Constellations in 1952 and named them after the ships of Christoper Columbus: EC-AIN (c/n 4550) *Santa Maria*, EC-AIO (c/n 4551) *Niña* and EC-AIP (c/n 4552) *Pinta*. They would be used on services to New York, with the first departing Madrid on August 3, 1954. After taking marketing advice the airline changed its name to Iberia, Líneas Aéreas de España.

In 1955, second president Jesús Rubio Paz stepped down after 14 years in office and was

BELOW: In 1935, the company purchased two Douglas DC-2s and legend has it that the contract was signed on a cigarette paper in Amsterdam
IBERIA

> ## "On September 22, 1946, a Douglas DC-4 departed Madrid/Barajas to establish the first regular service between Europe and South America"

Bebé on board

On a flight from Madrid to Havana on August 9, 1961, a baby was born on board – a first in Spanish aviation. Super Constellation EC-AIN (c/n 4550) *Santa Maria* was operating as normal after leaving the Azores, until flight attendant Lourdes Davisson asked if there was a doctor among the passengers, but there was not.

Heavily pregnant Juana Villarino was showing symptoms of distress and was moved to the first class area of the aircraft, which was hastily reconfigured into an improvised maternity ward. The birth occurred shortly after, somewhere over the mid-Atlantic, and Davisson recalled: "Everything went well thanks to the advice of Commander Galiana, a father of eight, who directed the midwifery, accompanied by flight attendants Ventura Caballero and Luis Sol. I will never forget that moment when the little girl, very pale with light eyes, cried."

The baby was named Loreto. Upon arrival at Havana, a doctor came aboard to examine mother and daughter and reported both to be in perfect condition. In 1983, Loreto would return to Spain, to honeymoon in Ibiza.

A decade after Loreto's marriage, in May 1993, another baby was born on a flight from Tokyo-Moscow-Madrid, aboard Boeing 747-200M EC-EEK (c/n 24071) *Garcia Lorca*. It was another girl, but this time the aircraft diverted to Frankfurt on medical advice. Another two airborne births also had happy endings, on services from Madrid to Nairobi and Madrid to Santo Domingo in the Dominican Republic.

ABOVE: Junkers Ju-52s were operated between 1937 and 1956, including EC-ABS **IBERIA**

replaced by Tomás Delgado, while passenger numbers increased to 577,036. The following year, the last three De Havilland DH-89 Dragon Rapides and last two Junkers Ju-52s were decommissioned. After the New York launch, the 'Super' – as it was informally known – began operating the Havana route. A menu from flight IB972 to Havana on July 3, 1956, was produced in Spanish, English, French, Italian and German, highlighting how quickly the airline was evolving. It offered Madrid-style soup, Florentine chicken breast, Duchess potatoes, American carrots, onions, pitta bread and coffee.

The following year – 1957 – saw the arrival of five new Convair CV-440 Metropolitan twin-props, offering 44 seats and a range of 1,200 miles. The 13th IATA General Assembly was held in Madrid to mark the 30th anniversary of Iberia's founding. The 'Super' was employed on services to Buenos Aires and San Francisco and, the year after, to Bogotá. As the 1950's drew to a close, Iberia aircraft had crossed the Atlantic more than 800 times.

The jet age begins

On December 9, 1960, the first Iberia office in New York opened at 518 Fifth Avenue. The same year, the connection to Tetuán ended, Son Bonet Airport in Mallorca ceased operations and services moved across the city to Palma de Mallorca/Son San Juan. Having purchased its first jets in July 1959, three Douglas DC-8-50s were delivered in the spring of 1961: EC-ARA (c/n 45617) *Velázquez*, EC-ARB (c/n 45618) *El Greco* and EC-ARC (c/n 45619) *Goya*. A service to Santiago in Chile was launched and, by the end of 1961, a total of 1,117,981 passengers had flown with the airline that year, which increased to 1,236,786 by the end of 1962.

The arrival of the DC-8s marked the beginning of Iberia's boom as 700 new staff joined the airline. Both crew and technicians visited the home of the Douglas company in California, where the ladies of Long Beach were built. At $8m a pop, it was a significant investment for the airline. »

RIGHT: Douglas DC-3 EC-ACX (c/n 19410) joined the fleet brand-new in 1944, but was written-off after departing Tenerife/Norte on September 16, 1966, crashing into the sea, with the loss of one of its 27 occupants **IBERIA**

ABOVE: On September 22, 1946, an Iberia DC-4 departed Madrid/Barajas to establish the first regular service between Europe and South America, arriving in Buenos Aires 36 hours and four stops later IBERIA

BELOW: Five new Convair CV-440 Metropolitan twin-props, including EC-AMT (c/n 403), arrived in 1957 and the type would stay in the fleet until 1972 IBERIA

On the ferry flight to Madrid on May 21with DC-8-52, EC-ARA (c/n 45617) *Velázquez,* a faulty oil seal in one of the engines was detected shortly after take-off. The aircraft had to return, but only after it had jettisoned most of its 88,000 litres of fuel, although technicians discovered the fault lay in the instrumentation rather than the engine. On May 29, after another ten test flights, it was finally welcomed to Madrid by a large crowd, despite the unseasonal rain. *El Greco* was delivered on May 31 and *Goya* on June 19, with a fourth, EC-ASN (c/n 45659) *Murillo,* delivered on October 4, 1962. The airline would eventually operate eight DC-8-50s, eight -60s and a solitary -70 variant.

At almost double the speed of the Super Constellation, and with its 146 seats offering almost double the passenger capacity, the DC-8 gradually replaced the 'Super' on transatlantic routes. It's revenue service with Iberia began on July 1, 1961, on the Madrid-New York route, before operating services to Caracas, San Juan, Mexico City, Havana and Buenos Aires.

During the same period, the airline also acquired the first of 20 Sud Aviation SE-210 Caravelles. The first, EC-ARI (c/n 107) *Albéniz,* arrived in February 1962, followed in the next few months by EC-ARJ (c/n 108) *Chap*i, EC-ARK (c/n 109) *Granados* and EC-ARL (c/n 110) *Falla.* The aircraft were named after Spanish composers and the fleet eventually totalled 20 of the type. It was inaugurated into the schedules on the Madrid-Rome route, then the Zurich route, and would stay with the airline until 1987.

During 1962, construction began on the company's new corporate headquarters at 130 Calle Velázquez in Madrid, while the fleet comprised 64 aircraft, including eight jets. A year later, the DC-8s begin flying to Lima, Peru, and a cargo division was introduced. It ended 1963 with 68 aircraft, including 12 jets. By the

ABOVE: Between 1962 and 1987, Iberia operated 20 Sud Aviation SE-210 Caravelles, each named after Spanish composers **IBERIA**

Come fly with me

On June 4, 1969, 17-year-old Armando Socarras Ramírez and 16-year-old Jorge Pérez Blanco enacted their plan to escape Cuba aboard Iberia's weekly flight 904 to Madrid, hiding in the landing gear compartment of the DC-8. The boys had previously observed aircraft movements at Havana/José Martí and knew the departure routine. Having climbed the perimeter fence and dashed across the grass, both tried to enter the same wheel well as the aircraft readied for its departure rollout. With insufficient space for two, Armando sped across the tarmac to the other main gear and climbed in. With cotton wool in his ears and some rope to secure himself, he prepared as best he could for the ten-hour flight to Madrid as the ground fell away and the doors shut. In the cockpit, a warning light signalled that the doors were not properly closed, so the process was repeated for a second time, surprising the stowaway in the process. Hours later and soon after parking in Madrid, Armando's barely alive body fell to the ground as the ice holding him in place quickly melted.

Statistically, 75% of such attempts end in the death of the stowaway, but Armando was one of the fortunate few to survive and was named 'Mr Popsicle' by Spanish doctors because he was covered in ice on arrival and suffered frostbite on a middle finger. It took several weeks before his hearing was properly restored, but there were no lingering medical issues and, after almost eight weeks, he was released from hospital. His co-conspirator, Jorge had fallen out before take-off and ended up in prison, while Armando eventually moved to the US.

end of the 1964, the last of the Bristol 170s had been retired and new routes to Milan, Brussels, Copenhagen and Stockholm were introduced.

On April 30, 1964, Iberia became the 17th airline to pre-order the Boeing 2707 SST, when it placed a $300,000 deposit for three aircraft – numbers 88, 92, and 96 – followed by another $300,000 advance payment soon after. In April 1971, the US Treasury returned the funds after the project was cancelled.

Around the same time, the airline was also operating the Carvair ATL-98, derived from the DC-4 by Freddie Laker's company, Aviation Traders. With capacity for five cars and 22 passengers, it was used on the Valencia-Palma de Mallorca route, with services to Morocco, Malaga and Nice never getting far beyond the drawing board. Iberia had two of its ageing DC-4s converted and operated services through Aviaco, which had been incorporated into Iberia in 1959, though it all came to an end in 1968.

The carrier signed a contract with Fokker on March 15, 1966, for eight 44-seat F28 Fellowships, equipped with side cargo doors, for later conversion into freighters. Flights from Madrid to Girona, Almeria and Oviedo were inaugurated and a flight simulator was

BELOW: On August 6, 1968, Iberia McDonnell-Douglas DC-8-63 EC-BMX (c/n 45930) *El Españoleto* was the first example of the type delivered to the airline, although it would be written-off on March 3, 1978 AIRTEAMIMAGES.COM/ CARL FORD

constructed at Barajas. By year end, the Super Constellations had been sold off and the 50 aircraft fleet included 21 jets: seven DC-8s and 14 Caravelles. The workforce comprised 9,000 people, and passengers numbers for the year stood at 2,255,171.

On June 30, 1967, the first Douglas DC-9-32, EC-BIG (c/n 47037) *Villa de Madrid*, arrived at Barajas Airport. Another six would follow before the end of the year, all named after Spanish »

"During 1962, construction began on the company's new corporate headquarters at 130 Calle Velázquez in Madrid"

LEFT: Lockheed L-1049G Super Constellation EC-AMP (c/n 4673) *San Juan* was delivered on July 8, 1957, and stayed with Iberia for a decade AIRTEAMIMAGES.COM/ATI COLLECTION

BELOW LEFT: Iberia McDonnell Douglas DC-9-32 EC-BIL (c/n 47084) *Ciudad de Zaragoza* was delivered on October 11, 1967, before transferring to Viva Air in January 1990. It is currently in storage AIRTEAMIMAGES.COM/ CARL FORD

towns and cities. The first of ten Fokker F-27 Friendships was also delivered, EC-BMS (c/n 10332) *Rio Ebro,* and it inaugurated the Madrid-Zaragoza route.

The new 'fried egg' logo was introduced and the livery became primarily a white and silver fuselage with a red cheatline. By the end of the year, passenger numbers had increased to 2.6 million, staffing totalled 9,210 employees and the 57 aircraft fleet included 33 jets, the first time the number of jets had exceeded 50%.

The following year, on August 6, 1968, the first of six Douglas DC-8-63s was delivered, although EC-BMX (c/n 45930) *El Españoleto* would be written-off on March 3, 1978, after landing long at Santigo de Compostela, aquaplaning off the runway and catching fire. All 222 occupants were safely evacuated.

Flights to New York expanded to 14 per week, and Montreal, Johannesburg and Dublin were added to the network. Before the year was out, a further two DC-8-63s had arrived: EC-BMY (c/n 45931) *Rosales* and cargo variant EC-BMZ (c/n 45988) *Los Madrazo.*

As the decade drew to a close, Iberia ordered its first 747s, starting a relationship with 'The Queen of the Skies' that would last until 2006.

"On August 3, 1954, flight 951 from Madrid/Barajas to New York/Idlewild commenced with a Lockheed L-1049G Super Constellation"

LEFT: On March 31, 1973, the first trijet joined the fleet when McDonnell Douglas DC-10 EC-CBN (c/n 46925) *Costa Brava* was delivered IBERIA VIA JOSÉ RAMÓN VALERO

BELOW: In 1964, Iberia became the 17th airline to pre-order the Boeing 2707 SST, when it made a $300,000 deposit for three aircraft, although the money was returned in 1971 after the project was cancelled BOEING

Welcome to the 1970s

Iberia experienced Spain's first hijacking on January 7, 1970, on a service from Madrid to Zaragoza. Fortified by alcohol and a toy pistol, Mariano Ventura Rodríguez made his move ten minutes before landing. Brandishing the toy, the 18-year-old computer science student demanded Convair CV-440-62, EC-ATG (c/n 349) be diverted to Albania. But after landing in Zaragoza as planned, and with the aircraft surrounded by police, Rodríguez abandoned his plan after being told he might be shot if anything happened to the crew or passengers. He was sentenced to six years in prison, serving three.

The airline moved into the widebody market on October 2, 1970, with the arrival of Boeing 747-156, EC-BRO (c/n 19957) *Cervantes*, to be followed »

> ### *"1977 was also the year the airline underwent a Landor facelift and launched what might be regarded as its 'classic' livery, which would be retained until 2013"*

on November 10 by EC-BRP (c/n 19958) *Lope de Vega*. The aircraft were delivered in a new livery to mark the new decade, with red and yellow regal bands running along the length of the fuselage and a quartered IB replacing the 'fried egg' logo. Both aircraft operated the flagship New York route and inaugurated the airline's inflight entertainment with the movie *Butch Cassidy and the Sundance Kid*. Three Fokker F-28 Fellowships were leased for crew training and cargo transportation: EC-BVA (c/n 11017) *Rio Arga*, EC-BVB (c/n 11019) *Rio Segre* and EC-BVC (c/n 11023) *Rio Jarama*.

A cargo terminal at Madrid/Barajas was opened in 1971, with capacity to handle 300,000 tonnes of cargo per year. The last Convair 440s left the fleet in 1972, while new routes to Panama and Guatemala were launched. On January 28, 1972, it joined the Atlas Group, a collective MRO organisation, which included Air France, Alitalia, Sabena and Lufthansa. Iberia's responsibility was for the overhaul of the JT9D-7Q and JT8D engines along with components for Concorde's Rolls Royce Olympus 593, DC-10s and Airbus A300s.

On May 2, 1972 the airline received its first Boeing 727-256, when EC-CAI (c/n 20592) *Castilla La Nueva* arrived in Madrid, followed soon after by EC-CAJ (c/n 20593) *Cataluña* and EC-CAK (c/n 20594) *Aragón*. Delivered with a flight simulator,

they were initially deployed on the puente aéreo (air bridge) between Madrid and Barcelona.

On March 31, 1973, the first trijet in the airline's history joined the fleet when McDonnell Douglas DC-10 EC-CBN (c/n 46925) *Costa Brava* was delivered, although it was written-off after hitting the approach lighting system (ALS) at Boston/Logan on December 17. There were no fatalities among the 168 occupants. The DC-10s operated on the Boston and Washington routes. Elsewhere, the last of the DC-3s entered retirement.

A 24-hour telephone information service called InforIberia was launched in August 1974 – a precursor to the modern call centre – and later renamed Serviberia. Two months later, in October, the Red Jackets service was created, with the mission to assist Iberia customers experiencing problems at airports. As the middle year of the

BELOW: Boeing 727-256 EC-CFD (c/n 20814) *Moriles Montilla*, delivered on February 6, 1974, had the honour of revealing the new Iberia livery at La Muñoza on November 3, 1977 AIRTEAMIMAGES.COM/ CARL FORD

ABOVE: Boeing 747-256B EC-DIB (c/n 22239) *Cervantes* was the fourth jumbo to join the fleet and second to carry the name. It would be the type that would take the airline into the 1980s and beyond AIRTEAMIMAGES.COM/ ISMAEL JORDA

decade rolled around, the network continued to expand, with new routes to Budapest, Warsaw, Istanbul, Athens, Dakar, Lagos, Panama City, Managua in Nicaragua and La Paz in Bolivia.

Further new routes in 1976 included Madrid to Reus and Badajoz (Spain), Monrovia (Liberia), Libreville (Gabon) and Abidjan (Ivory Coast). By the end of the year, passenger numbers had increased to 10.6 million, the number of employees to 19,254 and the fleet of 86 aircraft included 78 jets. For only the second time in its history, the airline posted a loss of almost 803m Pts.

On March 15, 1977, an armed Italian, Luciano Porcari, hijacked Iberia Boeing 727-256, EC-CBI (c/n 20603) *Asturias*, en route from Barcelona to Mallorca. Porcari had unsuccessfully tried to hijack an aircraft five years earlier, but this time he ordered the aircraft be flown to Abidjan in the Ivory Coast and demanded a $140,000 ransom and custody of his daughter, which he received but with just $16,000 in cash. The aircraft then flew to Casablanca, Seville, Turin, Zurich, Warsaw and back to Zurich, where its 36 passengers were released after police boarded the aircraft disguised as catering staff. Porcari was sentenced to a decade in prison.

BELOW: *Costa Brava*, shown here showcasing the relatively new 'fried egg' logo, was written-off on December 17, 1973, after hitting the approach lighting system at Boston/Logan IBERIA VIA JOSÉ RAMÓN VALERO

As the airline celebrated its half-century, the 33rd IATA Annual General Meeting was held in Madrid. The new international terminal at Madrid/Barajas Airport was opened and included Spain's first duty-free shop. New routes to Tehran, Lyon and Santander were launched.

This was also the year that Iberia underwent a Landor facelift and launched what might be regarded as its 'classic' livery, which would be retained until 2013. Munich-born Walter Landauer had set up his London-based company in 1941 and was quoted as saying: "Products are made in the factory, but brands are created in the mind." When Iberia came knocking, he had already produced liveries for Alitalia (1969), Singapore Airlines (1972), Hawaiian Airlines (1973) and Thai Airways International (1975). He would later be responsible for British Airways' 1984 livery.

El puente aéreo

The first rotation of the Madrid-Barcelona shuttle took place on November 1, 1974, on Iberia Boeing 727-256 EC-CAK (c/n 20594) *Aragón*. Barcelona resident Antonio Vilar was the first passenger to use a service that was completely new to Western Europe.

It operated from separate terminals at both airports, without reservation, and when there were enough passengers to fill the aircraft, boarding took place ten minutes prior to departure. Initially, there were 13 daily flights, offering 3,200 seats in either direction, flown by the DC-9s and 727s, most often utilised by business travellers making same-day round trips. In its first decade, it carried more than 11 million passengers.

By the end of the 20th Century, Iberia was operating around 45 daily flights on the route in each direction and would sometimes make a 747 or DC-10 available. It was only after the high-speed rail link between the two cities opened in February 2008 that flight numbers receded to around 25 per day.

The chosen design was an update of the 1970 iteration, coming from a longlist of 30 and a shortlist of four. The regal bands along the fuselage increased to three, one yellow and two red, and the logotype was made bolder. With aircraft still wearing 1967 and 1970 colours, the new livery was extended to all aircraft. It was Boeing 727-256, EC-CFD (c/n 20814) *Moriles Montilla*, delivered to the airline on February 6, 1974, that had the honour of revealing the new colours. It was presented to the public on November 3 at La Muñoza, the airline's new MRO hub at the southeastern periphery of Madrid/Barajas. The airline entered its second half-century emboldened and the president at that time, Manuel de Prado, stated that the new livery symbolised a complete remodelling of the airline. It would last for 36 years.

In the years that followed, Iberia purchased its first Airbus aircraft and continued to grow, as did it's home at Madrd/Barajas. In 2010, it would be merged into the International Airlines Group (IAG) with British Airways and, in 2013, its current livery was introduced.

As it approaches its 2027 centenary there is plenty more in the archive to be discovered. **A**

ATL90 *Accountant*
Counting the cost

POST-WAR, AIRCRAFT MANUFACTURERS WANTED TO REFLECT THE EXCITEMENT OF FLYING IN THE NAMES OF THEIR LATEST CREATIONS. IN BUILDING ITS FIRST AIRLINER, SOUTHEND'S AVIATION TRADERS TOOK A LEFT FIELD APPROACH, CHRISTENING IT THE ATL90 ACCOUNTANT AS IT WAS INTENDED TO KEEP AN AIRLINE'S FINANCE DEPARTMENT HAPPY AND ITS BOOKS IN THE BLACK. UNFORTUNATELY FOR FREDDIE LAKER, IT PUT ITS MANUFACTURER IN THE RED, AS STEPHEN SKINNER DETAILS

BELOW: Aviation Traders Limited's managing director, Freddie Laker, ATEL chief of flight test, Derryck Turner, World War Two ace Air Vice-Marshal Johnnie Johnson and ATEL chief test pilot, Laurence Stuart-Smith, with the Accountant at the 1957 SBAC Show

I n post-war aviation there were numerous attempts to replace the ubiquitous Douglas DC-3. As many as 20,000 Dakotas had been built and a large number were still in service. Early successors included the Vickers Viking and the Convair CV-240/340/440, but neither were powered by turboprops. The two types sold 163 and 1,181 units respectively, but both were out of production by the early 1950s.

Two more aircraft manufacturers decided that they would enter the market to replace the Dakota. These were Handley Page, whose Herald first flew in a four radial-engined form in August 1955, and the twin Rolls-Royce Dart-powered Fokker F27 Friendship, which took flight four months later. But they were not alone, there was a further contender – the ATL90 Accountant built by Aviation Traders.

Whereas Handley Page and Fokker were well-established aircraft manufacturers with many successful designs behind them, Aviation Traders (Engineering) Ltd (ATEL), based in Southend, was rather different. It had only been formed in 1947 by Freddie Laker, who later came to be regarded as one of Britain's great aviation entrepreneurs.

Initially, Aviation Traders dealt with scrapping war surplus aircraft, but then Laker fortuitously purchased 12 surplus Handley Page Haltons (civilianised Halifax bombers) and a large supply of spares from British Overseas Airways Corporation (BOAC).

Suddenly, in June 1948 when the Cold War was at its height, Soviet forces

LEFT: The nacelles of the Rolls-Royce Dart engines were mounted high above the wing, as a turboprop produces jet thrust as well as the traction from the propeller. This arrangement lifted the propellers high above the ground so that the undercarriage could be short

blockaded all land routes into West Berlin, and it was decided that the city must be supplied by the only way possible – by air. Laker's Haltons were pressed into use as freighters during the year-long Airlift, proving an exceptionally profitable investment which set ATEL on its feet and made Freddie Laker extremely wealthy.

With the end of the airlift, Aviation Traders modified surplus Avro Yorks and in 1953 purchased ten of the heavily-flawed Avro Tudors from the government; the company carried out a large number of modifications on them in the hope of improving their safety record and performance. These types were then employed for trooping and cargo flights by Freddie Laker's airline, Air Charter. ATEL also expanded into the aircraft component manufacture, making the wing centre-sections for Bristol Freighters and later installing wing spar modifications on the type at its Stansted airport hangars.

Laker had proved very adept at developing his business, but his acumen escaped him when it came to his next project – developing a replacement for the Dakota. The DC-3 was able to carry 21-36 passengers, 14 passengers as a VIP transport, or 2,300cu ft of freight and could operate from poorly surfaced runways. Laker envisaged that despite the competition an inexpensive turboprop replacement would

BELOW: The ATL90 Accountant, designed and built by Aviation Traders, was one of several aircraft that billed themselves as a replacement for the venerable Douglas DC-3 Dakota ALL IMAGES KEY PUBLISHING UNLESS STATED

receive many orders, for example from British European Airways (BEA) which operated 44 examples during the 1950s. To help him achieve his aim, in 1952 he employed Toby Heal, former assistant chief designer at Hunting Aircraft, along with several other of his former colleagues who formed a small design team at Aviation Traders' Stansted base.

All systems go

In 1953, the Accountant got the green light from Freddie Laker and Heal's team moved to ATEL at Southend Airport.

The Accountant was promoted at the 1953 Farnborough Air Show and cross-section illustrations showed it with a side-opening nose allowing for the straight-in loading of cars or 15 stretchers or lengthy pieces of freight.

However, ATEL did not have the market to itself, as Fokker was starting work on the F27 Friendship and Handley Page was already working on the Herald – at this time, a four-engined aircraft powered by Alvis Leonides Major radial engines.

In 1954, Toby Heal patented what he called the 'tensioned skin' system of construction. In earlier wood and fabric aircraft, much of the

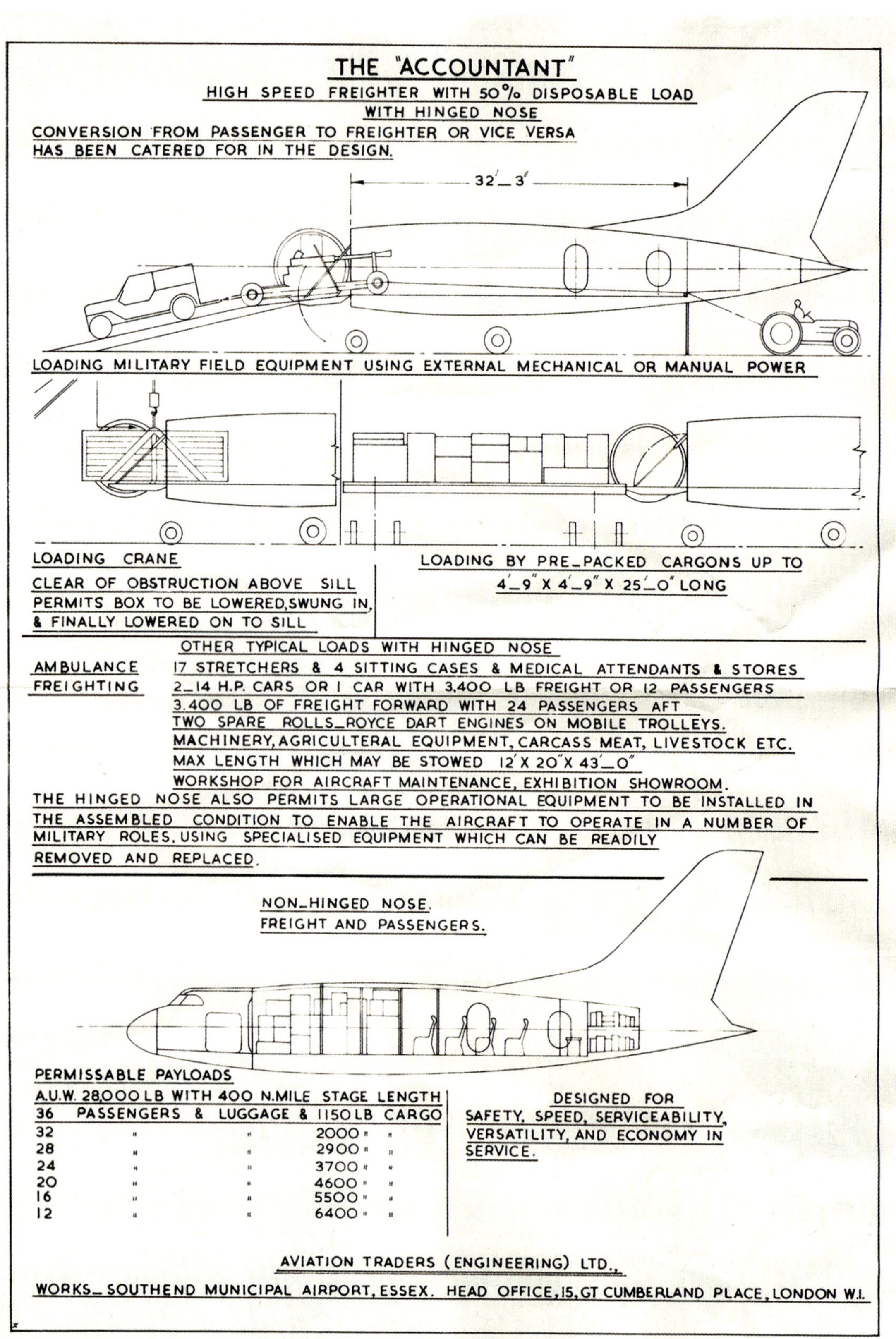

LEFT: The Accountant was designed with a "50% disposable load conversion from passenger to freighter or vice versa"

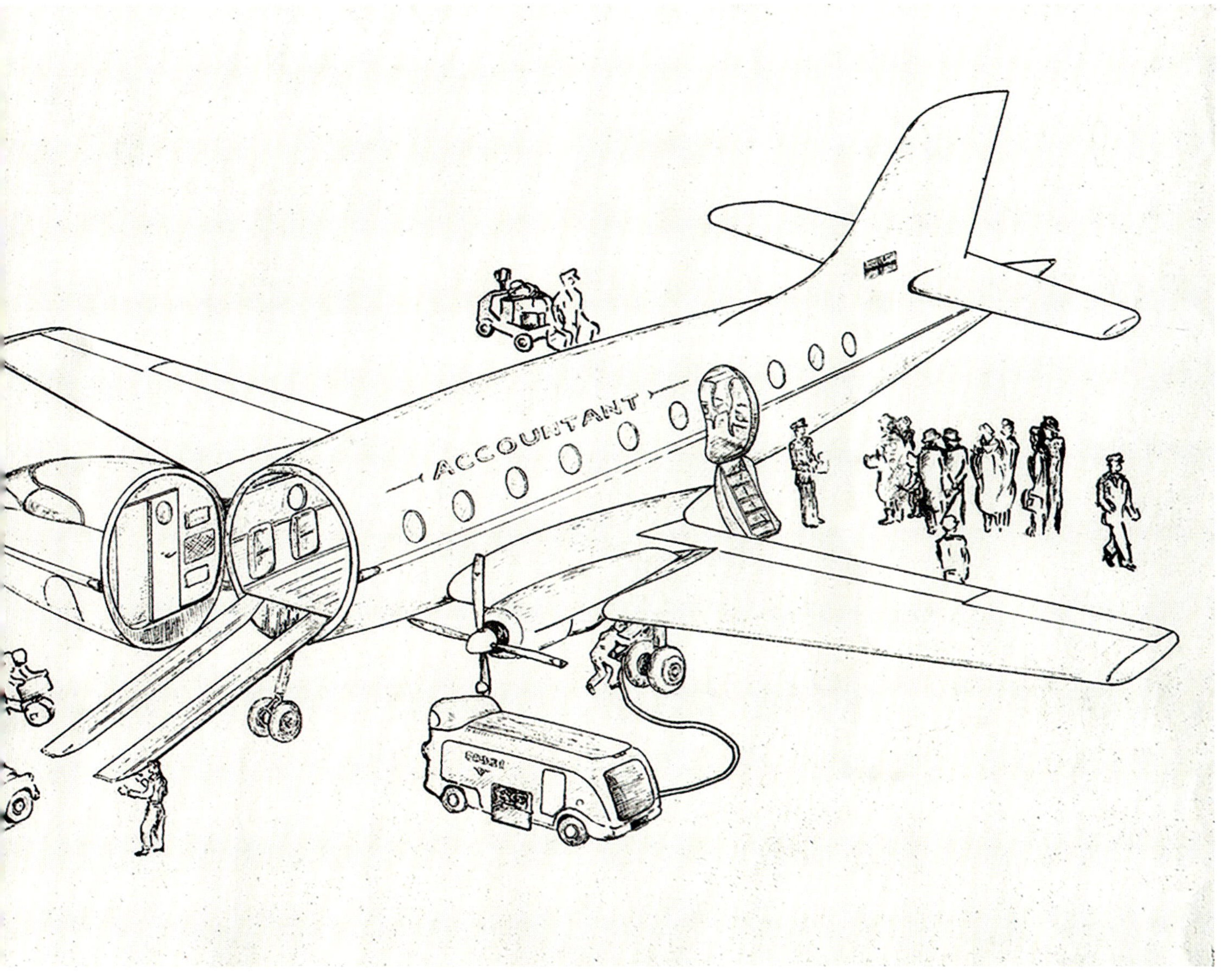

stiffness of the airframe was provided by the fabric covering, which was tightened by doping. Heal's intention was to achieve the same with the metal skin.

For the method to work, the aircraft's fuselage had to be designed so its outer skin curved in two directions at once, both round its circumference and along its length.

Because of the metal skin's contribution to the strength of the structure, it could then be considerably lightened, so increasing the aircraft's payload – giving it appeal to an accountant. So, the design was nicknamed the Accountant, as it was deemed to be more efficient and more profitable than the Dakota. Soon, the name stuck.

The Accountant was a low-wing design powered by Rolls-Royce Dart turboprops, able to accommodate up to 36 passengers, cruising at 240kts at 25,000ft. It was a simple, rugged aircraft designed to operate from relatively under-developed airfields yet with a range of 1,300nm. Though the aircraft had a broadly conventional design, it had several distinct features. The curved fuselage shape was slightly reminiscent of the Constellation.

As production aircraft could be fitted with the swing-nose to allow for straight-in loading of freight or cars, this feature necessitated an aft nosewheel position, giving the aircraft a rather ungainly appearance on the ground. The Dart nacelles were mounted high above the wing as a turboprop produces jet thrust as well as the traction from the propeller, so is most efficient if the exhaust path is straight. This arrangement lifted the propellers high above the ground, so the undercarriage could be short.

A stretched Mark II Accountant was intended to have accommodation for up to 42 passengers to compete with the Handley Page Herald and Fokker Friendship, and the Mark III would

ATL-90 Accountant Facts	
Manufacturer	Aviation Traders
First flight	9/7/1957
Number built	1
Length	62ft 1in
Height	25ft 3in
Wingspan	82ft 6in
Wing Area	632sq ft
Empty weight	16,961lb
Max takeoff weight	32,000lb
Max speed	295mph
Range	1,800nm
Powerplant	x2 Rolls-Royce Dart Turboprop
Flight crew	2

»

ABOVE: On display at the 1957 Society of British Aerospace Companies (SBAC) Show at Farnborough. Laker had ensured that the prototype had gained enough hours to be allowed to take part in the flying displays

BELOW: The nose landing gear of the Accountant was set further back than usual to accommodate the type's unique swing nose

have had greater fuel capacity and longer range. As costs mounted the Accountant's name seemed all the more worrying to Laker, who joked that the Mark II version should be named the Auditor and the Mark III the Receiver.

Freddie Laker showed his bargaining skills when obtaining the Dart engines for the prototype from Rolls-Royce. He asked Rolls' chairman Lord Hives for the loan of two Darts, but was refused as Hives claimed Laker owed Rolls-Royce money. Laker responded that if Rolls-Royce checked it would find the opposite was the case: it owed Laker money. So ATEL got the Darts on loan. By mid-1956, slow progress was being made with the construction of a prototype. Though three prototypes were originally projected, only one was ever completed in full.

Competition mounts

Meanwhile, competing airliners for the Dakota replacement market took to the air in 1955. The Herald flew in a four piston-engine arrangement in August and the Friendship in November 1955. However, Handley Page soon realised its prospect of orders had evaporated; airlines had become accustomed to reliable turboprop airliners such as the Viscount which was already in service and with the Friendship now in the air. Freddie Laker had presciently not made such a mistake

ABOVE: It impressed the crowds with the flying displays, although some of the trade visitors were disappointed in the type's odd look

BELOW: On the afternoon of July 5, 1957, the ATL-90 Accountant made its maiden flight from Southend. Due to buffeting and stability issues, the aircraft only remained airborne for 21 minutes

as Handley Page and had chosen Dart turboprops from the start.

At the end of April 1957, the Accountant was rolled out quite unceremoniously from its Southend hangar. It was practically complete with its Dart engines in place, but without propellers fitted. It was painted in an attractive red and white livery bearing the B-class registration, G-41-1. The aircraft was not furnished nor soundproofed, though it had an instrumented flight test observer's position in the cabin. As a precaution prior to its maiden flight, it was fitted with a large anti-spin parachute in an extended tail cone.

With Laurence Stuart-Smith, the company's chief test pilot, and Derryck Turner, chief of flight test, at the controls, the Accountant carried out taxi trials on Southend airport's newly constructed main runway on July 5. Stuart-Smith was an experienced wartime pilot who had been trained at the Empire Test Pilots' School at Boscombe Down, Wiltshire. On the afternoon of July 9, 1957 everything was ready for the maiden flight and Aviation Traders Ltd (ATL) engineers, employees and many others gathered to watch the event. Freddie watched from Southend Airport control tower. During the flight, the Accountant experienced severe stability and buffeting problems. As a result, Stuart-Smith remained at a low altitude extremely close to the airfield and landed after only 21 minutes in the air. As the crew disembarked, they received applause from onlookers and Freddie was there to congratulate them on their efforts. There was no mention of how troublesome the flight had been.

The prototype then remained on the ground for five weeks. During this time, it was decided to adjust the tailplane incidence in the hope of curing some of the aircraft's problems. On August 12 after two taxi runs it took to the air once more, but again was soon back on the ground when the buffeting reoccurred. It was so serious that at some speeds the instrument panels were unreadable and the tailplane was visibly vibrating. From flight four, wool tufts and streamers were attached to the engine nacelles and wing trailing edge. The source of the buffeting was traced to the rear of the engine nacelles and the Dart jet pipes were then extended to the rear. The performance improved and it was now registered as G-ATEL – one of the earliest $\gg$

examples of a bespoke registration, certainly not commonplace as it is today.

Further flights took place as it was necessary for the ATL90 to have ten hours in the air to appear at that September's Society of British Aerospace Companies (SBAC) Show at Farnborough. Laker was desperate to have his airliner in the flying display in the hope of earning some orders. (The SBAC Shows were, in those days, held annually and restricted to British-made aircraft.)

It impressed the crowds during its daily demonstration flights, though on one landing the brakes were burnt out owing to a misunderstanding on the flight deck. Some of the trade visitors were disappointed by the look of the aircraft with its large tail, odd nosewheel undercarriage and prominent engine nacelles, so unlike the Viscount's unobtrusive mountings. Laker's response was that Bristol had sold more than 200 of its far-from-beautiful Type 170 Freighter.

Though the Indian Air Force and other customers showed interest, no orders were received. It was clearly impossible to sell an aircraft with no delivery date and none in production.

As Laker's company lacked both the skills and infrastructure to test and manufacture the aircraft, he tried to persuade other manufacturers such as Gloster, which was short of work, to take on these tasks – without success.

Hunting Percival carried out an assessment of the Accountant and came to the view that substantial redesign would be necessary to sort out the flaws in aerodynamics and systems. Building a second, much-modified prototype

ABOVE:
AVIATIONANCESTRY.CO.UK

LEFT: Historians continue to ponder whether the Accountant had the potential to transform Southend into an aviation hub

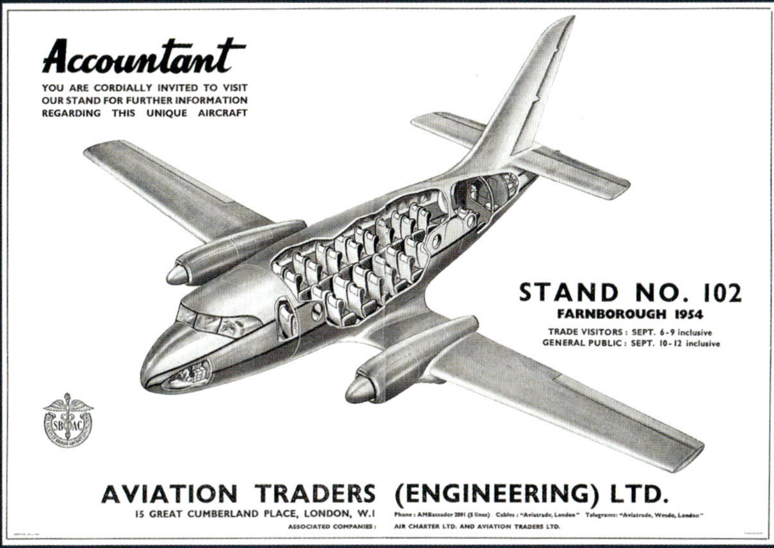

clouds were gathering. The type was making its namesake its nemesis. On January 10, 1958, the Accountant took off on its 30th and final sortie.

After 50 flying hours since its maiden flight, the project came to an end. Despite the best efforts of Laker and his engineers, there were no production plans, no orders and no firms wishing to take it on. They had achieved a lot, but it was far beyond the resources of what today would be deemed a maintenance, repair and overhaul (MRO) provider.

The Accountant was financed out of ATEL and Air Charter's profits, but with no profit in sight, Laker's fellow directors wanted the project halted. In January 1958, it was axed. Workers were laid off and G-ATEL was parked outside the hangars in which it was built. Its engines removed and returned to Rolls-Royce. It was scrapped in February 1960.

of the larger 40-seat Accountant Mk.II able to compete with the Fokker Friendship and the re-engined Handley Page Dart-Herald was far beyond the company's resources and it would not have been ready until 1960, with first deliveries the following year.

The Friendship had not only amassed orders but entered service in 1957 with the Herald starting its airline career in 1959, so it was impossible for the Accountant to make up lost ground.

Gathering clouds

In the meantime, the flight test programme continued and on the Accountant's 13th sortie, Air Charter's chief test pilot, Bob Langley joined Stuart-Smith at the controls. A Laker-owned airline, Air Charter would have been an obvious customer for the ATL90. As the aircraft kept on flying, the costs continued rising and dark

'Avro Accountant'

Laker bore a grudge for many years against the Avro (later Hawker Siddeley) 748, which he regarded as a copy of the Accountant and, according to some sources, referred to it as the "Avro Accountant" – the configuration of the two is broadly similar. In contrast to Laker's aircraft, 382 Hawker Siddeley 748s were built including 89 by licence in India, some of which are still in service. Another similar-looking Dart-powered aircraft is the Grumman Gulfstream I. The American-built type saw 200 sales, only serving as executive transport.

When the registration certificate of G-ATEL was returned to the Aircraft Registration Board (now the Civil Aviation Authority), Laker requested use of it on the next ATEL type, the Carvair, but was refused. Aviation Traders Ltd went on to convert 21 DC-4s into Carvairs but never again would it build a new aircraft.

BELOW: Laker bore a grudge for many years against the Avro (later Hawker Siddeley) 748, which he regarded as a copy of the Accountant

AVIATIONANCESTRY.COM

Thirty years of easyJet

SINCE ITS INCEPTION IN 1995, EASYJET HAS GROWN INTO THE LARGEST SCHEDULED CARRIER IN THE UK AND ONE OF THE BIGGEST LOW-COST CARRIERS IN EUROPE. WITH ARTWORK FROM ROLANDO UGOLINI, WE TAKE A LOOK BACK AT THE HISTORY OF THE LUTON-BASED AIRLINE

The airline took to the skies on November 10, 1995, with a flight from London/Luton to Glasgow piloted by Captain Fred Rivett. The inaugural service was operated by a Boeing 737-204 on lease from GB Airways. Along the side of the fuselage was the airline's booking telephone number in bright orange Pantone 021C, with the airline's name in its Cooper Black font on the tail, a change from the traditional red, white and blue liveries around at the time ALL IMAGES ROLANDO UGOLINI

When easyJet launched operations, it did not have its own Air Operators Certificate (AOC), so GB Airways provided the airline's first two aircraft on wet-lease. The pair of Boeing 737-204s – G-BECG (c/n 21335) and G-BECH (c/n 21366) – had started life with Britannia Airways in 1977

In May 1996, easyJet received its first Boeing 737-3Y0, G-EZYA (c/n 23498). This allowed the airline to launch its first international flights to Amsterdam on April 24, 1996, followed by Barcelona and Nice as additional 737-300s arrived. These were flown under Air Foyle's AOC until easyJet was finally awarded its own in October 1997

In March 1998, the airline purchased a 40% stake in ailing Swiss carrier TEA Switzerland AG for 34m Swiss francs, before buying the remaining shares in April 1999, rebranding it as easyJet Switzerland and moving its operations from Basel to Geneva

In July 1998, easyJet ordered 15 next-generation Boeing 737-700s, welcoming its first example, G-EZJA (c/n 30235), in October 2000. This followed an order for 17 more in March that year. The airline would go on to operate a total of 33 of the type between 2000 and 2011

In December 2001, easyJet offered £390m in cash and shares to purchase its biggest rival, the former BA low-cost subsidiary Go. The offer was rejected, but easyJet persisted and, on May 16, 2002, a £384m deal was accepted. Overnight, easyJet became Europe's biggest low-cost carrier, with a fleet of 54 737s (compared to Ryanair's 44) and almost doubled its route network from 45 to 81, with new bases at London/Stansted, Bristol and East Midlands

On December 16, 1999, easyJet commenced flights at London/Gatwick with a service to Geneva before establishing a base at the West Sussex facility in February 2002. Since then, the airline has grown to become the airport's biggest operator

In November 2002, the airline's founder and chairman, Sir Stelio Haji-Ioannou, announced his intention to step down. This came a month after the airline had signed a landmark deal for 120 CFM-powered Airbus A319 jets, with options on a further 120, following a hard-fought battle between the European plane-maker and Boeing

The airline received its first A319 in September 2003, when HB-JZB (c/n 2043) was delivered to its Swiss subsidiary. In April 2007, easyJet welcomed its 100th example, and a special livery was applied to A319-111 G-EZBR (c/n 3088) to mark the occasion. The carrier would go on to become the world's largest customer for the A319, having purchased a total of 172 examples since the first order

On October 25, 2007, easyJet purchased GB Airways. The £103.5m deal meant easyJet would become the largest airline at London/Gatwick overnight, boosting capacity by 30% and controlling almost a quarter of all slots. It would also give the LCC a ready-made base at Manchester airport, with six routes and two based aircraft

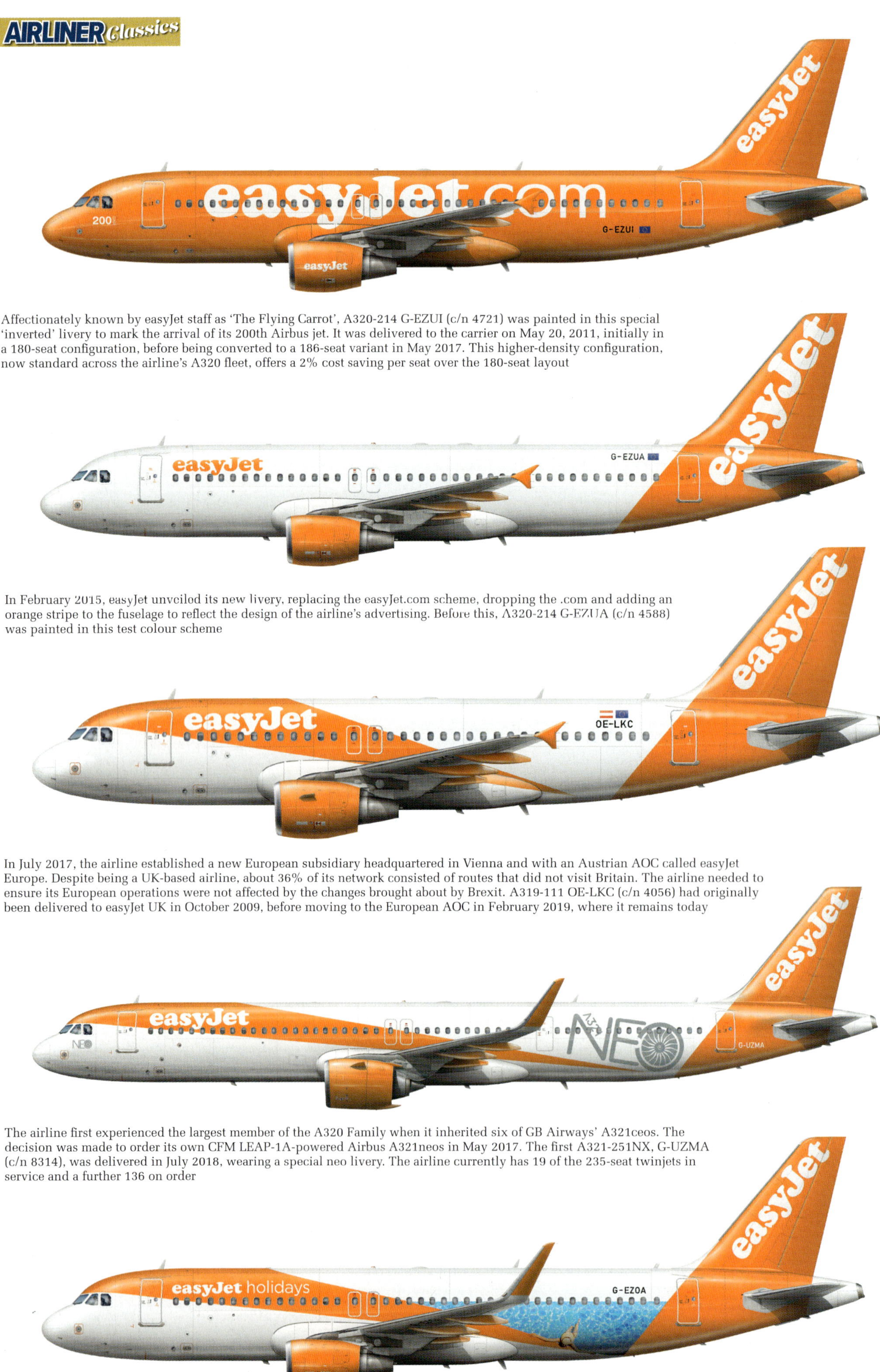

Affectionately known by easyJet staff as 'The Flying Carrot', A320-214 G-EZUI (c/n 4721) was painted in this special 'inverted' livery to mark the arrival of its 200th Airbus jet. It was delivered to the carrier on May 20, 2011, initially in a 180-seat configuration, before being converted to a 186-seat variant in May 2017. This higher-density configuration, now standard across the airline's A320 fleet, offers a 2% cost saving per seat over the 180-seat layout

In February 2015, easyJet unveiled its new livery, replacing the easyJet.com scheme, dropping the .com and adding an orange stripe to the fuselage to reflect the design of the airline's advertising. Before this, A320-214 G-EZUA (c/n 4588) was painted in this test colour scheme

In July 2017, the airline established a new European subsidiary headquartered in Vienna and with an Austrian AOC called easyJet Europe. Despite being a UK-based airline, about 36% of its network consisted of routes that did not visit Britain. The airline needed to ensure its European operations were not affected by the changes brought about by Brexit. A319-111 OE-LKC (c/n 4056) had originally been delivered to easyJet UK in October 2009, before moving to the European AOC in February 2019, where it remains today

The airline first experienced the largest member of the A320 Family when it inherited six of GB Airways' A321ceos. The decision was made to order its own CFM LEAP-1A-powered Airbus A321neos in May 2017. The first A321-251NX, G-UZMA (c/n 8314), was delivered in July 2018, wearing a special neo livery. The airline currently has 19 of the 235-seat twinjets in service and a further 136 on order

The carrier launched its easyJet Holiday subsidiary in November 2019 and added a special livery to A320-214 G-EZOA (c/n 6412). This aircraft had initially been delivered to the airline in December 2014

Oh, I do like to be beside the seaside

FOR OVER 80 YEARS, BLACKPOOL AIRPORT WELCOMED A VARIETY OF COMMERCIAL AIRLINES, BRINGING HOLIDAYMAKERS TO THE SEASIDE TOWN. LEE CROSS TELLS THE STORY OF THE FACILITY UP TO ITS CLOSURE TO PASSENGER FLIGHTS IN 2014

Blackpool Airport can trace its history back to October 1909, when the airfield held the UK's first official public flying meeting on a specially laid out site at Squires Gate, a district in South Shore. More than 200,000 spectators watched legendary French airman Henri Farman perform his unique flying display, while Henri Rougier brought his Voisin biplane. In 1910, the Lancashire Aero Club staged a second aviation meeting between July and August, and the first commercial airmail flight took place on August 13, 1910. By 1911, the site had become a race course and was later used as a military hospital during World War One until 1924.

Operations resumed in April 1933, when Blackpool and West Coast Air Services began commercial flights to the Isle of Man, Manchester and Liverpool. Passengers could then connect from Liverpool to London and the Southwest. The Air Ministry requisitioned the airfield in 1938 and three runways were laid to support the squadrons based there during World War Two, with the new RAF station officially opening on October 23, 1939. The RAF trained 769,673 cadet pilots at Blackpool during the war due to accommodation availability.

Between September 1940 and October 1945, Vickers-Armstrong produced 2,584 Wellington Bombers at Squires Gate following the construction of a shadow aircraft factory in the northeast corner of the airfield. This was taken over in 1951 by the Hawker Aircraft Company, which began building its Hunter jets until 1958, after 374 had been made.

Post-war years

On September 6, 1946, the airport reopened for civilian use, with ⟫

ABOVE: Between September 1940 and October 1945, Vickers-Armstrong produced 2,584 Wellington Bombers at Squires Gate following the construction of a shadow aircraft factory in the northeast corner of the airfield KEY COLLECTION

BELOW: Blackpool Airport is located on the Fylde coast, Lancashire, between the towns of Blackpool and Lytham St Annes AIRTEAMIMAGES.COM/ SIMON WILLSON

RIGHT: In 1980, British Island Airways was merged with Air Anglia, Air Wales and Air Westward to form a new independent carrier, AirUK AIRTEAMIMAGES.COM/ THE SAMBA COLLECTION

flights by Isle of Man Air Services resuming to Isle of Man/Ronaldsway airport. These flights and their fleet of de Havilland Rapides were subsequently taken over by the newly formed British European Airways (BEA) on January 31, 1947.

Independent carrier Lancashire Aircraft Corporation (LAC) began operating from Blackpool, adding services to the Channel Islands and Southport. In 1950, they took over BEA's flights and added more services to Leeds, Glasgow and Birmingham, along with North West Airlines, who shared the scheduled route to Ronaldsway.

As jet aircraft became increasingly popular, the airport extended its runway in 1952 to facilitate these new airliners. In 1956, a new control tower was built to handle the increasing number of airfield movements. In the same year, LAC became a subsidiary of Silver City Airways and the airline continued expanding at Blackpool with up to 35 weekly rotations to the Isle of Man during the peak 1958 summer season.

The route was considered the airline's 'pot of gold', especially after the Isle of Man Steam Packet Company suspended its Fleetwood sailings in 1961. LAC responded by adding a

BOTTOM: British United Island Airways (BUIA) was created in 1968 as a subsidiary of BUA to cover all services across the Irish Sea and to the Channel Islands AIRTEAMIMAGES.COM/ THE SAMBA COLLECTION

BELOW: Henri Rougier in his Voisin biplane at the Blackpool Aviation Meeting in 1909, with helpers pushing or pulling on the wing leading edge KEY COLLECTION

virtually half-hourly 'ferry service' at weekends using de Havilland Herons and Bristol Wayfarers. In 1961, Blackpool flights to Ronaldsway accounted for 48% of all movements.

In 1958, Aer Lingus partnered with Silver City and began flying from the airport to Dublin. At the beginning of 1962, it was announced that Silver City would become part of British United Airways (BUA), a new airline managed by Sir Freddie Laker.

Regional renaissance

British United Island Airways (BUIA) was created in 1968 as a subsidiary of BUA to cover all services across the Irish Sea and the Channel Islands. They quickly made Blackpool a hub for their northwest operations and year-round flights to the Isle of Man and Belfast continued. BUIA also took over the Dublin rotation from Aer Lingus in 1969 and established an on-site engineering facility.

On January 16, 1980, British Island Airways (the 'United' had been dropped in 1970 when British Caledonian took over BUA) was merged with Air Anglia, Air Wales and Air Westward to form a new independent carrier, AirUK.

Sadly, the severe recession that crippled the UK in the early 1980s hit the new airline hard and management decided to close the engineering base and drop many of its routes. Dublin and Belfast were cut, although the recently formed Spacegrand Aviation promptly took these over. The once-booming hop across the Irish Sea to Ronaldsway was also slashed to just once daily and the airport suffered a significant drop in passenger numbers.

In 1982, AirUK joined forces with British Midland to create Manx Airlines, which immediately took »

BELOW: Blackpool and West Coast Air Services operated commercial flights to the Isle of Man, Manchester and Liverpool
BLACKPOOL AIRPORT

over the Belfast and Isle of Man routes and added a seasonal rotation to Jersey. In the summer of 1983, Spacegrand added a thrice-daily Isle of Man flight to its network in direct competition with Manx, which had cut the route to a daily flight.

Manx Airlines had put its newly delivered Fokker F27 on the route, believing that passengers would prefer the space and comfort of a larger aircraft. They were wrong. Passengers wanted the frequency that Spacegrand offered. Manx subsequently leased an eight-seat Piper Navajo Chieftain to increase frequency to four times daily. The decision proved popular and, a year later, the airline upgraded the service to a DHC-6 Twin Otter provided by partner Loganair, who would also occasionally operate the Belfast route. Spacegrand was eventually merged with Jersey European Airways in 1985, and the newly formed airline continued to operate from Blackpool for several years.

On March 26, 1984, Genair, a small independent airline that provided feeder services for British Caledonian under the Commuter brand, extended its London/Gatwick to Liverpool service to Blackpool. Sadly, the carrier was placed into administration in July 1984 and dropped the route.

Throughout the years, the airport has welcomed various charter carriers from across the UK and Europe, operating holiday flights and bringing competitors to the dance competitions held at the iconic Blackpool Tower Ballroom. To help handle these charters, a new terminal was opened in 1995 next to the old wooden building, which was demolished in 1996.

Jet2's arrival

In 2005, Jet2.com became the first major low-cost carrier to base an aircraft at Blackpool, creating 50 new jobs and boosting passenger numbers. The airline initially launched flights to Alicante, Amsterdam, Belfast, Faro, Malaga, Murcia, Prague and Tenerife South, flying two Boeing 737-300s. They would also offer a seasonal link to Jersey.

Competition immediately came from Monarch Airlines, which commenced a thrice-weekly route to Malaga in the summer of 2005. The service lasted just a year, with the carrier blaming low passenger numbers and increased competition from Jet2.

In 2007, Jet2 cancelled the Prague and Amsterdam services, citing low passenger numbers. Despite this, 2007 was when the airport was at its peak, handling more than half-a-million passengers annually.

On July 18, 2008, Jet2 revealed that it planned to suspend its daily link to Belfast International for the winter. A dip in passenger numbers and rising oil prices had taken their toll on the service. The route was restored in March 2009 and lasted until the end of the summer 2013 season, when it was dropped permanently.

Strained relations

Jet2's relationship with the then-owners of Blackpool Airport was sometimes tense. The airport had been arguing over the timings of a number of the airline's flights, claiming that late-night and early-morning departures were costly and unsustainable, forcing the airfield to operate at a loss.

BELOW: Manx Airlines took over the Belfast and Isle of Man routes from AirUk and added a seasonal rotation to Jersey
AIRTEAMIMAGES.COM/ CAZ CASWELL

prevent Jet2 from operating outside its published opening of 0700-2100hrs. A court case ensued, which Jet2 eventually won, allowing operations to continue as they had done previously.

In June 2012, the airline announced plans to serve Dalaman, Ibiza and Lanzarote from May 2013. This coincided with the carrier revealing they would upgrade one of their Boeing 737-300s to a larger -800 series, providing extra capacity on its bucket-and-spade routes. On May 21, 2014, Menorca was added to the schedule, followed by Reus a year later.

Homegrown talent

Manx Airlines became part of BA Connect (BAc) in February 2006. After a series of mergers and name changes, the 'new' airline looked to remodel itself as a low-cost carrier. Part of this move meant unprofitable routes were dropped, including all services from Blackpool. Enter British North West Airlines, which stepped in with a BAe Jetstream 31 to fill the gap on the Isle of Man and Belfast/City rotations, albeit on a relatively short-lived basis.

Following British North West Airlines' demise, flights to the Isle of Man were taken over by Citywing, flying up to three times a day, with an onward connection to Belfast/City. Citywing introduced low fares on these routes, leading to an increase in passenger numbers in January 2007.

With passenger numbers rising, another new carrier operating as Jetstream Express, »

Matters came to a head in October 2010, when two flights were forced to divert to Manchester late one evening after the facility was closed by management. The airport had also threatened to

LEFT: An Astraeus Airlines Boeing 737-7BX G-STRC (c/n 30736) awaits its next load of charter passengers outside Blackpool's small terminal building KEY-TONY DIXON

BELOW: To help handle these charters, a new terminal was opened in 1995, next to the old wooden building, which was demolished in 1996 KEY COLLECTION

ABOVE: Ryanair began serving Blackpool in May 2003, with routes to Dublin, London/Stansted and Girona
AIRTEAMIMAGES.COM/SIMON WILLSON

introduced flights in 2007 to Belfast City, Aberdeen and Southampton. Two Jetstream 31s were based at the airport to support the operation. However, the services ended in June 2007 as the routes proved unviable.

Controversy

In 2008, infrastructure group Balfour Beatty, which already owned Exeter and Londonderry airports, purchased a 95% stake in Blackpool from previous owners CityHopper Airports LTD for £14m. The previous owners, who had also run Wolverhampton Airport and Biella Airport in Italy, had purchased the share from Blackpool Council, who retained the remaining 5%.

However, in January 2009, the new owners, looking to recoup some of their costs, decided to implement a £10 fee for all departing passengers aged 16 or over. The Airport Development Fee was a controversial decision, with many travellers angry at the additional charge. The fee was paid at a ticket machine in the terminal, with proof of payment needed to pass through security.

One particularly unhappy airline was Ryanair, which announced on November 25, 2008, that it would withdraw all flights from January 5, 2009. The carrier had operated from Blackpool

since May 2003 with routes to Dublin, London/Stansted and Girona, carrying more than 1.3 million passengers. Aer Arran, operating under the Aer Lingus Regional banner, stepped in to replace Ryanair on the Dublin rotation until it was axed in 2014.

The new owners set to work at redeveloping the airfield. Several changes were implemented during 2011, including redeveloping some taxiways and relocating the airport's fire services to a more central position, away from their previous location north of the airport fuel farm.

Danish Air Transport also announced plans to launch a new twice-weekly route to Albert-Picardie Airport (BYF) in northern France in April 2012. Sadly, the flights were cancelled before the launch.

Closure

Despite the additional fee implemented to "save the airport", in August 2014, Balfour Beatty revealed it would put Blackpool up for sale. On October 7, it was announced that the airport would close, with £34m in debt and the loss of 100 jobs. Owners blamed falling passenger numbers and their poor contract with the its primary carrier, Jet2.

Jet2 had been performing well since its launch, with rumours circulating about new routes and a third based aircraft. Sadly, any plans the airline had were quashed, and the carrier was forced to move its 26 rotations per week to Manchester from October 9, 2014.

Two years after the closure, Jet2's then-CEO Philip Meeson told the *Blackpool Gazette* that they had no plans to return even if Blackpool were to restore commercial flights: "If I'm realistic, I don't think the door will reopen, sadly. That's the realism, I think. We did not want to leave. We were very disappointed to leave. But now we're gone, we're gone. We're very, very sorry. We're very disappointed that it happened."

The final commercial service was operated by Citywing, with flight V9117 departing for the Isle of Man on October 15, 2014. **AC**

BELOW: Jet2 was forced to move its 26 rotations per week from Blackpool to Manchester from October 9, 2014, signalling the beginning of the end for passenger flights at the airport
KEY-MARTIN NEEDHAM

FOCNK
AIR FRANCE
VICKERS VISCOUNT
QUATRE TURBO-PROPULSEURS ROLLS-ROYCE DART

For four decades, Air Afrique's aircraft embodied pan-African optimism – the belief that newly independent nations could take to the skies together and, by doing so, announce their arrival on the world stage. Between 1961 and 2002, Air Afrique's story would mirror that of Africa itself: ambitious, inspiring and ultimately undermined by politics and economic forces that refused to co-operate.

An airline for Africa

The 1950s and early 1960s were years of transformation across the African continent. France's former colonies were stepping into independence and each was eager to display the trappings of nationhood: flags, anthems, currencies and airlines. Yet unlike many Anglophone states that fractured their colonial carriers into smaller national ventures, the Francophone bloc decided to stay united.

On March 28, 1961, 11 governments – Benin (then Dahomey), Burkina Faso (Upper Volta), Central African Republic, Chad, Republic of the Congo, Côte d'Ivoire, Mauritania, Niger, Senegal, Gabon and Cameroon – met in Yaoundé and signed the Treaty of Yaoundé, thereby creating Air Afrique. The plan was radical for the time: a single, multinational flag carrier representing all members equally, headquartered at Abidjan/Port Bouët Airport in Côte d'Ivoire. Each state would hold a share, while France would provide technical support and aircraft through Air France, Union de Transports Aériens (UTA) and the French Development Agency (FDA). The member states held a collective share of 68.4%, while the French flag carrier and FDA held 11.8% and 8.9%,

Wings of Africa

THOMAS HAYNES REVISITS THE RISE AND FALL OF AIR AFRIQUE, A BOLD EXPERIMENT IN MULTINATIONAL AVIATION THAT SUCCUMBED TO POLITICAL INFIGHTING AND FINANCIAL COLLAPSE

respectively. The remaining shares were held by private investors.

UTA supplied the initial fleet of Douglas DC-4s on lease. The first five – F-BBDA (c/n 042909), F-BBDF (c/n 042938), F-BBDI (c/n 042941), F-BBDK (c/n 042943), F-BJHH (c/n 042985) – arrived in August 1961 and were re-registered locally in Côte d'Ivoire as TU-TBF, TU-TBG, TU-TBH, TU-TBE and TU-TBI, respectively, in April 1962.

They were crewed at first by UTA pilots and engineers, while African recruits underwent training in Paris and Abidjan. On August 1, 1961, Air Afrique began domestic operations with its DC-4s. Within months, they were joined

BELOW: Air Afrique accepted McDonnell Douglas DC-10-30, TU-TAM (c/n 46892), on June 19, 1975
AIRTEAMIMAGES.COM/ WOLFGANG MENDORF

by more capable Douglas DC-6Bs, with the first, F-BGVV (c/n 043557), arriving on lease from UAT in October 1961. On October 15, 1961, an Air France Lockheed Constellation flew the Paris-Port Etienne-Dakar-Abidjan-Cotonou-Douala route on behalf of Air Afrique, inaugurating the carrier's long-haul operations.

Flying into the jet age

In January 1962, Air Afrique joined the jet age when it deployed two Boeing 707s, leased from Air France, on the Paris-Dakar-Abidjan and Paris-Douala-Brazzaville routes, cutting journey times dramatically. That year, the airline also became »

ABOVE: Air Afrique's first Douglas DC-8-53s, TU-TCA (c/n 45670) and TU-TCB (c/n 45671), arrived from the Long Beach, California factory on October 19, 1963, and January 10, 1964. TU-TCB is seen here engineless in storage at Luxembourg in 1984 AIRTEAMIMAGES.COM/ WOLFGANG MENDORF

a member of the International Air Transport Association (IATA), a step that enhanced its global recognition. In a bid to acquire its own metal, Air Afrique ordered two examples of the rival Douglas DC-8 in December 1962. The DC-8-53s, TU-TCA (c/n 45670) and TU-TCB (c/n 45671), arrived from the Long Beach, California factory on October 19, 1963, and January 10, 1964 – lead times today's airlines can only dream of.

As the network expanded, so did ambition. In April 1964, Air Afrique won approval from US authorities to connect several African countries with the United States. In May the following year, in a codeshare deal with Pan Am, it became one of the first African airlines to launch services to New York, inaugurating its transatlantic services initially via Dakar. For many West Africans, this represented the ultimate statement of independence: their own airline name on the departures board beside Air France, Pan Am and

ABOVE: Air Afrique bolstered its long-range DC-8-30 fleet towards the end of the 1960s, sourcing TU-TCD (c/n 45627) from UTA AIRTEAMIMAGES.COM/ THE SAMBA COLLECTION

BELOW: On February 28, 1973, Air Afrique took delivery of its first McDonnell Douglas DC-10-30, registered TU-TAL (c/n 46890) and christened it *Libreville* AIRTEAMIMAGES.COM/ PHILIPPE NORET

BOAC. The carrier would evolve to operate its own New York services in 1971.

By 1966, Air Afrique was transporting around 300,000 passengers every year, linking most member capitals with Paris, Geneva and Marseille.

In September 1967, the airline received two French-built Sud Aviation SE 210 Caravelle 11Rs and a mixed passenger-cargo 10R. The trio's arrival resulted in the sale of two DC-4s. The Caravelles were deployed on intra-African routes, replacing the DC-6s.

Air Afrique bolstered its long-range Douglas DC-8-30 fleet towards the end of the 1960s, followed by the addition of the DC-8-55CF Jet Trader combi freighter variant. These gave Air Afrique true intercontinental reach and cargo carrying capability, ushering in a decade of growth. By the early 1970s, DC-8s were operating from Abidjan and Dakar to Paris, Marseille, Rome, Geneva, Zurich and New

York, while the Caravelles handled regional hops across West and Central Africa.

In a somewhat random decision, Air Afrique ordered two Japanese-built NAMC YS-11 turboprops. Little is known about the type's involvement with the carrier, with only one example, TR-LPJ (c/n 2128), having been tracked down as arriving in December 1970.

Each aircraft in the fleet carried a name from one of the member states – *Brazzaville*, *Cotonou*, *Niamey*, *Libreville* – a subtle reminder that Air Afrique belonged to them all. Abidjan's airport, newly expanded, became the main technical base, while Dakar/Yoff served as a northern gateway to Europe and the Americas.

Trijet revolution

The true leap forward came in 1973. On February 28, Air Afrique took delivery of its first McDonnell Douglas DC-10-30, registered TU-TAL (c/n 46890) and christened it *Libreville*. It was the first widebody airliner operated by a West African carrier and its arrival signalled that Air Afrique had joined the big league. Two weeks later, on March 2, TU-TAL made its first appearance in Dakar and by mid-month it was flying the trunk route of Paris-Dakar-Abidjan. The DC-10's combination of range and capacity allowed the airline to consolidate services, replacing multi-stop DC-8 routings with single-sector flights. By 1975, the airline was employing about 3,700 staff and operating three Caravelles, five DC-8s and a DC-10 across a network of 22 African cities and eight European destinations.

The DC-10 proved an instant hit with both passengers and crews. A second DC-10-30, TU-TAM (c/n 46892), arrived on June 19, 1975, but was immediately leased to Thai Airways for a year until May 20, 1976, when it returned to Air »

BOTTOM: Air Afrique's third DC-10-30, TU-TAN (c/n 46997), was delivered on August 10, 1979 AIRTEAMIMAGES.COM/ WORLD AVIATION ARCHIVE

BELOW: In 1979, Air Afrique became the first African airline to order Airbus aircraft, signing for a trio of A300B4s. The first, TU-TAO (c/n 137) arrived in May 1981, followed by another, TU-TAS (c/n 243), in July 1983 and the third, TU-TAT (c/n 282), in September 1984 AIRTEAMIMAGES.COM/ RALF MEYERMANN

Afrique, bolstering its trijet fleet to two examples. A third DC-10, TU-TAN (c/n 46997), followed on August 10, 1979.

Passenger figures climbed steadily and, for a time, Air Afrique was profitable. The green-tailed DC-10s became ambassadors of a confident new Africa, their distinctive roar over the Atlantic earning them affection among spotters in Paris and New York. However, the rise of Air Afrique wasn't without stumbling blocks. In 1971, Cameroon withdrew from the consortium, followed by Gabon in 1977. They each wanted to establish their own airlines for political reasons – a desire to distance themselves from France – and thus blocked Air Afrique from accessing their markets. The exit of the two countries followed the integration of Togo into the consortium in 1968.

Enter Airbus

In 1979, Air Afrique became the first African airline to order an Airbus aircraft, signing up for a single A300B4, intended the fly the Dakar-Paris route, and two A310s. The order was later adjusted to just a trio of A300B4s. The first, TU-TAO (c/n 137), arrived in May

BELOW: During the early 1980s, Air Afrique leased a pair of Boeing 727-200s from JAT Yugoslav Airlines, including 727-2H9, YU-AKL (c/n 22666) AIRTEAMIMAGES.COM/ WOLFGANG MENDORF

1981, followed by another, TU-TAS (c/n 243), in July 1983 and the third, TU-TAT (c/n 282), in September 1984. They soon took over key routes between Abidjan, Dakar and Paris. These widebody twins offered lower operating costs and greater reliability, giving the airline a much-needed technological boost.

For a short time, Air Afrique operated a single Boeing 747-200F, which was delivered brand-new from the factory in October 1980. The jumbo, TU-TAP (c/n 22169), left the fleet in March 1985 and was leased to Cargolux. The airline also briefly operated a passenger configured 747-123, N9667 (c/n 20106), between September and December 1985 and a subsequent example, LX-KCV (c/n 20102), between October 1986 and January 1987. Although impressive on the ramp, the jumbo's economics were crippling and they were returned to their lessors quickly. Nevertheless, they added glamour to an already eclectic fleet and underscored Air Afrique's bold ambitions.

Political crosswinds

The oil crises of the 1970s and early 1980s sent fuel prices soaring, while member governments pressed the airline to maintain unprofitable domestic links as a matter of prestige. Each capital wanted to see the green tail on its apron, regardless of load factors. The principle of consensus – that every shareholder had a veto – made cost-cutting virtually impossible.

A policy of 'Africanisation', introduced in the early 1980s, replaced many expatriate staff with nationals of member states. In theory, this was a necessary step towards full sovereignty, but in practice it introduced a new layer of political patronage. Key managerial posts were distributed according to nationality rather than merit and rival governments jostled for influence.

The fragile structure cracked in 1984, when a strike over proposed pay cuts escalated into a full-scale crisis with 117 pilots and technicians, including 56 French expatriates, being dismissed after refusing to return to work. The disruption cost the airline millions and damaged its reputation for reliability.

Although the Ivorian director-general Aoussou Koffi later managed to cut the deficit, the sense of drift deepened. By the late 1980s, debt had   »

LEFT: The airline dabbled with the Boeing 747 in the early 1980s, including 747-123, LX-KCV (c/n 20102), between October 1986 and January 1987, but couldn't make the economics work. The jet is seen here in April 1987 at London/ Gatwick with its next operator, Caribbean Airways
AIRTEAMIMAGES.COM/ KEITH BLINCOW

BELOW: By 1998, four of the airline's A310s had been seized by creditors
AIRTEAMIMAGES.COM/ TMTAVIATION

ABOVE: The Lockheed L-1011 TriStar made a brief appearance in Air Afrique's fleet. Between October 1989 and July 1995, the carrier leased four examples for periods ranging from one month to one year, namely N185AT (c/n 193C-1052), which was leased from American Trans Air between October 1989 and October 1990 AIRTEAMIMAGES.COM/THE SAMBA COLLECTION

reached $250m, staff numbers exceeded 5,000 and productivity was falling. The 'Africanisation' of the airline was also completed with Africans occupying all top administrative positions.

Rescue attempts

The early 1980s also saw the rise of stiff competition for Air Afrique on its flagship routes. Competition from other national and international airlines such as Ghana Airways, Nigeria Airways, Air France and UTA squeezed revenues on key routes.

In 1989, member states adopted a plan spearheaded by the African Development Bank and several shareholder governments which proposed an $180m bailout, tied to a reduction of 2,000 staff and strict performance targets, including member governments restricting the competitive environment by limiting traffic rights granted to other airlines in the region. Implementation of the plan proved elusive as many states simply failed to contribute their share.

By 1990, the fleet comprised three A300B4s, one DC-8-63F, and three DC-10-30s. That same year, former Air France executive Yves Rolland-Billecart was appointed chairman and chief executive. Experienced and determined, he introduced a series of reforms: cutting 1,600 positions, tightening financial controls and modernising the fleet. His decision to standardise the fleet around Airbus A300s and A310s angered unions, who accused him of favouring French manufacturers, but from an operational perspective it made sense. The first of four brand new A310-300s, TU-TAC (c/n 571), arrived on April 29, 1991, followed by TU-TAD (c/n 651)

in August 1992, TU-TAE (c/n 652) in September 1992 and TU-TAF (c/n 671) in August 1993. The arrival of the A310s gave the airline a medium-haul aircraft ideal for European and North African services.

Devaluation and debt

The fatal blow came on January 12, 1994, when the CFA franc – the shared currency of the airline's member states – was devalued by 50% against the French franc. In the years since 1990, the airline had borrowed millions of dollars to procure the four A310s and launch new services. Its aircraft leases and loans were denominated in hard currency and the debt burden doubled overnight. Around two-thirds of expenses, including fuel, spares and insurance, were payable in dollars or francs, while ticket revenue continued to flow in the newly weakened CFA.

The result was devastating. By 1998, Crédit Lyonnais, Dresdner Bank and Midland Bank had seized four A310-300s as collateral, removing a third of the passenger fleet. Flights were cancelled at short notice, maintenance schedules were disrupted and the once-proud green tails began disappearing from European skies. France and several member governments stepped in with emergency funding on multiple occasions, but these injections merely postponed the inevitable. Each bailout came with promises of reform that were quietly ignored once the crisis passed. »

BELOW: Air Afrique took delivery of ex-Lufthansa Airbus A310-304, TU-TAZ (c/n 595), on August 12, 1999. The jet is seen here in Hamburg on August 9, ahead of delivery and still wearing its German registration D-AIDM
AIRTEAMIMAGES.COM/ TMTAVIATION

ABOVE: The A300B4-600R shared the two-crew electronic flight deck technology of the A310
AIRTEAMIMAGES.COM/ RALF MEYERMANN

Change at the top

In 1997, the board turned to Sir Harry Tirvengadum, the man credited with building Air Mauritius into a success story. If anyone could save Air Afrique, it was him. Within months, he grasped the scale of the challenge.

Each shareholder insisted that flights to its capital continue, regardless of profitability, and few paid their bills. Tirvengadum tried to streamline the route map, negotiate with creditors and improve on-time performance, but entrenched political interests resisted. The carrier's bureaucracy – 32 directors spread across a dozen states – made rapid decisions impossible.

Meanwhile, external shocks compounded the problem. The civil conflict in the Republic of the Congo forced the suspension of services for nine months, costing around 13 billion CFA francs. In December 1999, a military coup in Côte d'Ivoire disrupted operations at Abidjan, the airline's main base, adding to the chaos.

By the turn of the millennium, Air Afrique's finances were in freefall. Debt had climbed to $458 million and maintenance backlogs grew as spare-parts suppliers demanded cash up front. A World Bank audit in 2000, conducted by the American consultancy Simat, Helliesen & Eichner, found that the company's accounting systems had effectively ceased to function the previous year. Local stations were collecting revenue independently, ticketing control had broken down and nearly 40% of passengers were travelling free of charge – often utilising their political connections.

The audit also revealed that the airline now employed around 4,000 people to operate just six serviceable aircraft. For comparison, easyJet, then a relative newcomer in Europe, flew 21 aircraft with 1,400 staff. Payroll consumed nearly all income, leaving nothing for investment or fuel.

The final descent

In an effort to attract private investment, the World Bank organised a meeting of shareholders in Washington DC in 2000. The resulting 'Washington Plan' proposed restructuring, followed by partial privatisation and a strategic partnership – most likely with Air France. But both the unions and several governments rejected the idea, fearing job cuts and a loss of national influence.

By mid-2001, the situation was irretrievable. Creditors began repossessing aircraft, fuel suppliers demanded payment in advance and strike threats re-emerged. On February 7, 2002, after 41 years of operation, Air Afrique was formally declared bankrupt. Its remaining DC-10s were ferried to storage and its offices across Africa and Europe fell silent. The network fragments were soon absorbed by other carriers: Air Ivoire, Air Senegal International and later Air Côte d'Ivoire inherited elements of the route structure, while Air France quietly took over the profitable Paris links.

For many West and Central Africans, the disappearance of Air Afrique felt personal. It had connected their capitals when few others could and its aircraft had carried generations of travellers to school, business and family. At its best, it was a symbol of what co-operation could achieve; at its worst, it was a lesson in how politics can bring down even the most well-intentioned enterprise. **A**

BELOW: In 1995, Air Afrique took delivery of two brand-new Airbus A300B4-604Rs, including TU-TAH (c/n 744), which was leased from ILFC
AIRTEAMIMAGES.COM/ ANDREW HUNT

World's first
widebodied twinjet

THE DECISION TO LAUNCH A PAN-EUROPEAN WIDEBODIED AIRCRAFT PROGRAMME WAS ANNOUNCED AT THE 1969 PARIS AIR SHOW. THIS FOLLOWED DISCUSSIONS BETWEEN THE FRENCH, GERMAN AND UK GOVERNMENTS REGARDING A COLLABORATION BETWEEN THEIR RESPECTIVE AIRCRAFT MANUFACTURERS TO BETTER COMPETE WITH THE US GIANTS THAT WERE DOMINATING THE MARKET AT THE TIME. THE PROJECT BECAME THE GROUNDBREAKING A300, AND HERE WE TAKE A LOOK AT THE WORLD'S FIRST WIDEBODY TWINJET AND ITS EQUALLY SUCCESSFUL SMALLER SIBLING, THE A310

RIGHT: A European operator of the A300 was Finnair, which had a pair of Airbus A300B4-203FFs between 1990 and 1998. The aircraft, OH-LAA (c/n 299) and OH-LAB (c/n 302), were originally delivered to Finnish charter carrier KarAir in December 1986 and March 1987, respectively. However, in April 1990, following Finnair's acquisition of a 90% stake in the charter airline and its subsequent reorganisation as a scheduled domestic operator, the A300s were transferred to the Finnair fleet KEY COLLECTION

BELOW: The prototype Airbus A300B1, F-WUAB (c/n 001), took to the skies on October 28, 1972, from the manufacturer's Toulouse/Blagnac facility, a day later than planned due to unfavourable weather conditions. At the controls were Aérospatiale's senior test pilot Max Fischl and the head of flight test, Bernard Ziegler. They were joined by two flight engineers and an observer. The flight lasted an hour and 25 minutes, during which the aircraft reached a maximum altitude of 14,000ft and speed of 185kt AIRBUS

ABOVE: During the public unveiling ceremony of the world's first widebody twinjet on September 28, 1972, Alpha Bravo was positioned with Concorde 02. The aircraft had actually been rolled out a month earlier and had gone on to complete several ground tests **AIRBUS**

ABOVE: German flag carrier Lufthansa signed a deal for three A300B2s in 1975 and received its first, D-AIAA (c/n 021), on February 9, 1976, in a special ceremony at Hamburg/Finkenwerder. The General Electric GE CF6-50-powered jet was christened *Garmisch-Partenkirchen*, after a small Alpine ski town in Bavaria, Southern Germany. The airline would go on to operate 29 A300s, retiring its last example in 2009. Alpha Alpha was later sold to French regional carrier Air Inter **LUFTHANSA**

ABOVE: Monarch Airlines was one of only two UK operators of the A300, the other being Laker Airways. The London/Luton-based carrier had first agreed a deal for four General Electric CF6-powered jets in 1988, the first of which arrived in April 1991. The final example – and indeed the final European passenger example – G-OJMR (c/n 605) was retired on April 13, 2014, with a special farewell flight from London/Gatwick to Birmingham
KEY-MARTIN NEEDHAM

ABOVE: The A300 was eventually deemed too big for Lufthansa's requirements. After first introducing the A310 in April 1983, the airline used the type to replace its A300s. A total of 25 were operated, consisting of 13 A310-200s and 12 of the larger -300 series **KEY COLLECTION**

A selection of Airbus A300/A310s awaiting delivery around the Aérospatiale building in Toulouse. Two A310s were destined for Swissair, along with an A300 for Thai Airways and an A300 for the United Arab Emirates (Abu Dhabi Amiri Flight). All four wear their Airbus F- test registration
CREATIVE COMMONS BY-SA 4.0 ETH LIBRARY ZURICH, IMAGE ARCHIVE / LBS_SR04-000460

ABOVE: The A310 entered service with joint launch customer Swissair in April 1983. Plans for the A300's smaller sibling had been announced in April 1978, with orders from the Swiss flag carrier and Lufthansa. The type featured various upgrades from the A300, including a two-crew glass cockpit KEY COLLECTION

ABOVE: Pakistan International Airlines (PIA) placed an order for four A300B4s in July 1979 and received its first example in March 1980. In June 1991, it received its first A310-300 AP-BDZ (c/n 585). The fourth example to be delivered was AP-BEQ (c/n 656), which is seen here at Birmingham Airport KEY COLLECTION

ABOVE: Air Transat was the last airline in North America to retire the Airbus A310, with its last example leaving the fleet in March 2020, due to the drop in air travel following the COVID-19 pandemic. G-GSAT (c/n 600) had started its life with Emirates in February 1992, before moving to Kenya Airways and finally joining the Canadian leisure carrier in August 2001 KEY COLLECTION

ABOVE: Six A310s were ordered by Singapore Airlines for deliveries to start in October 1984. The deal with Airbus meant the airline could trade in its A300 fleet and replace them directly with the A310s. Remaining with the airline until June 2000, when it was transferred to Hapag-Lloyd, 9V-STL (c/n 363) was delivered in March 1985 CREATIVE COMMONS BY-SA 4.0 ETH LIBRARY ZURICH, IMAGE ARCHIVE / LBS_SR04-013333

ABOVE: CSA Czech Airlines operated four Airbus A310-300s. The first two arrived in 1995, followed by another two in 2004. They became the airline's first widebodies and replaced Ilyushin Il-62s on services to North America and Asia. All four examples were configured in a two-class layout with 21 business class recliner seats in a 2-3-2 configuration and 188 economy seats in a 2-4-2 layout KEY COLLECTION

THE DESTINATION FOR
AVIATION ENTHUSIASTS

Visit us today and discover all our latest releases

Laker Airways Skytrain McDonnell Douglas DC-10-30, G-BGXE
(c/n 47811), was delivered in January 1980, the first longer-range
example of the trijet for the airline, which had previously operated
the -10 model. Pioneered by Sir Freddie Laker, the airline's Skytrain
service took off on September 26, 1977, after five years of legal
battles on both sides of the Atlantic. Flights from London/Gatwick
initially served New York/JFK, while Los Angeles was added a year
later AIRTEAMIMAGES.COM/ATI COLLECTION

Here comes

HELIOS AIRWAYS WAS THE FIRST INDEPENDENT AIRLINE IN CYPRUS, BREAKING THE MONOPOLY HELD BY THE ISLAND'S FLAG CARRIER AND GOING UP AGAINST THE LIKES OF OLYMPIC AND BRITISH AIRWAYS. LEE CROSS SPEAKS TO FOUNDER, ANDREAS CHRISTODOULIDES TO REVEAL THE STORY BEHIND THE GROUNDBREAKING AIRLINE AND THE TRAGEDY THAT LED TO ITS CLOSURE

For years, Cyprus Airways had dominated the aviation market of the small island nation in the southern Mediterranean and, by the mid-1990s, it was carrying more than a million passengers each year. However, times were changing and the liberalisation of air travel across Europe, coupled with the island's desire to join the European Union, meant the flag carrier's monopoly would soon be challenged.

One airline that planned to capitalise on the new open skies policy was Trans European Airways (TEA). TEA could trace its history back to 1970, with the formation of TEA Belgium. From then, several new subsidiaries were established across the continent, including France, Turkey, Switzerland, Italy and the UK.

In 1994, a TEA team, led by Cypriot entrepreneur Andreas Christodoulides, along with Marcus Seiler and Yiannis Anamakedonas, looked at establishing a Greek subsidiary to operate domestic routes from a base in Athens. Unfortunately, at the time, the aviation market in Greece was dominated by the fiercely protected Olympic Airways and, after three years, the project was abandoned.

Instead, the team looked to Cyprus, as Christodoulides explained: "Our plan was simple: let's go to Cyprus to develop a charter airline. Not to compete with Cyprus Airways and its subsidiary Eurocypria, but to capture some of the market from the foreign airlines that had started flying to the island. We wanted to bring a new dynamic image to Cyprus. To create jobs. To increase tourism, with bases planned at both Larnaca and Paphos."

At the time, the state-owned carrier and its charter arm held a modest 15% of the lucrative market to and from the island, with the rest coming from overseas carriers. The proposed venture aimed to carry 50,000 passengers in its first year, growing to 195,000 by year two and corner around 2.5% of the market for itself during its first season of operation.

In September 1998, Christodoulides' dream became a reality. With strong financial backing from his family, together with Swiss and Cypriot shareholders from the shipping, tour operations and aviation sectors, the plan to establish Cyprus' first private airline got underway.

"The airline was registered as Aphrodite Airways – Aphrodite being the goddess of love and beauty who came from Cyprus," Christodoulides said. "But the name was already registered. So we came up with the idea of Helios Airways – Helios being the Greek god of the sun."

The early years

The team then looked to source an aircraft. "We wanted to commence operations with the Next Generation Boeing 737-800," Christodoulides said. "It was the hottest property on the market. But we had a dilemma: to start up or not start up, as there was a backlog with deliveries of the type at the time."

RIGHT: Boeing's in-house design team created the airline's eyecatching livery. It featured azure blue and 'Helios' titles in billboard-style lettering along the fuselage, along with the face of the Greek god emblazoned on the tail ALL IMAGES ANDREAS CHRISTODOULIDES COLLECTION UNLESS STATED

BELOW: Helios Airways was founded in September 1998 and commenced operations between Larnaca and London/Gatwick on May 26, 2000, becoming the first privately owned airline in Cypriot history AIRTEAMIMAGES.COM/ CARL FORD

the sun!

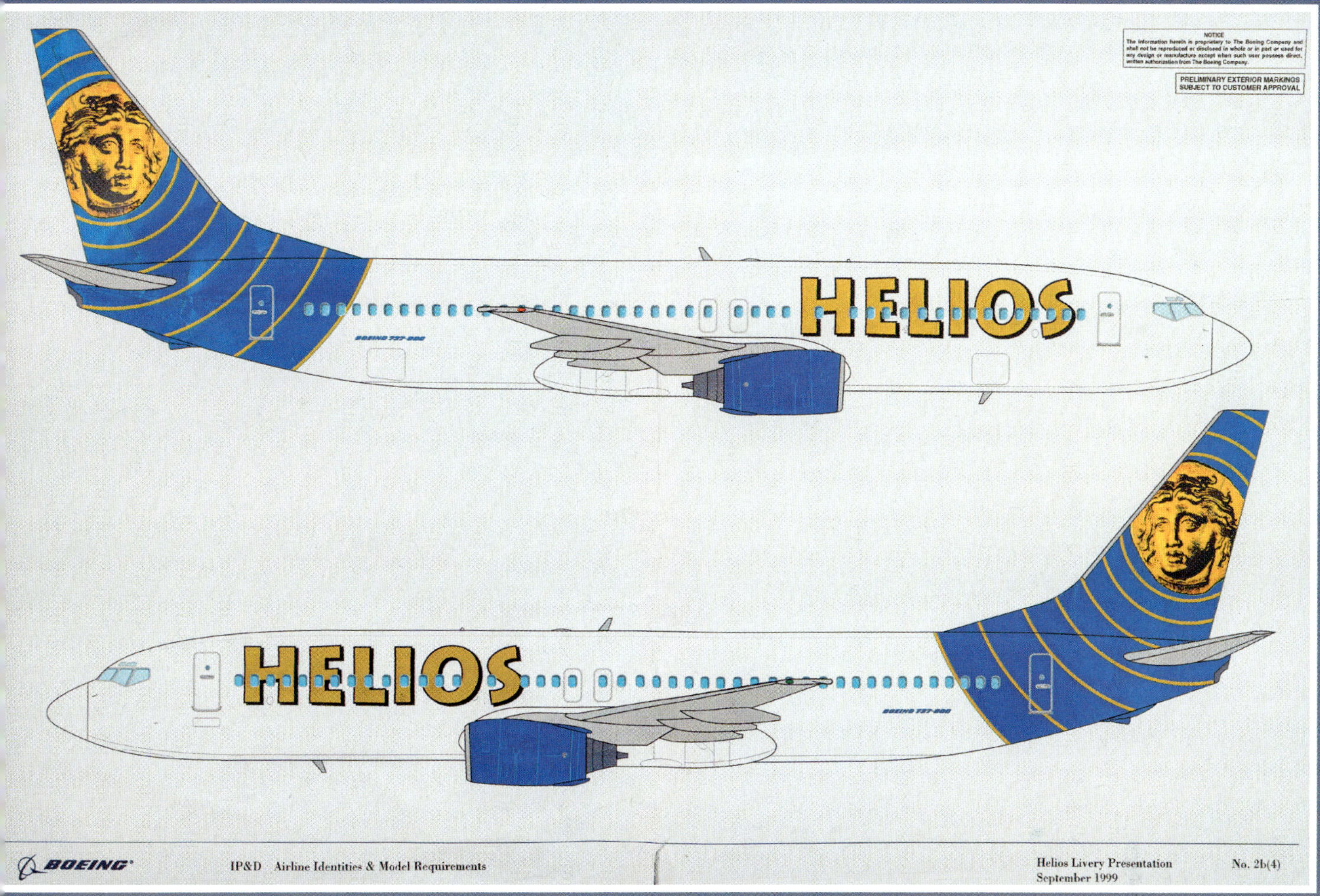

After discussions with lessor GE Capital Aviation Services (GECAS), the new operator was offered a ten-year-old Boeing 737-4Y0, 5B-DBG (c/n 24682), which had previously flown for Futura Airways. This would be used for a year, while Helios awaited the arrival of a pair of brand-new 737-800s.

Named Athena, the aircraft, looking resplendent in the carrier's distinctive livery of azure blue and 'HELIOS' titles in billboard-style lettering » along the fuselage, along with the face of the Greek god emblazoned on the tail, touched down at the airline's Larnaca base on May 17, 2000. A week later, Helios received its Air Operator's Certificate (AOC) from the Cyprus Directorate of Civil Aviation.

With an aircraft and an AOC, Helios was ready to start operations. On May 26, 2000, to much fanfare, its first flight took off from Larnaca, bound for London/Gatwick. Flights to London/Luton followed two days later. Demand quickly grew, prompting the start-up to expand its Gatwick service from three to five flights per week, operating at around 90% capacity.

During its inaugural season, the new carrier offered charter flights to eight UK airports, including Humberside, Aberdeen and Norwich, all brand new destinations for Cyprus.

Other routes included Paris/Charles de Gaulle, Milan/Bergamo, Basel, Zurich, Budapest, Warsaw and Zakynthos.

Growth and expansion

Following a successful first season, Helios received its highly anticipated pair of Boeing 737-86Ns in time for the summer 2001 schedule. The first, 5B-DBH (c/n 30806) *Zela,* named after Christodoulides wife, was handed over during a special rollout ceremony at the manufacturer's

ABOVE: The airline's first aircraft was a ten-year-old Boeing 737-4Y0, 5B-DBG (c/n 24682), which had previously flown for Futura Airways

LEFT: Initially, the team had wanted to christen the carrier Aphrodite Airways, after the goddess of love and beauty who came from Cyprus, but the name was already registered

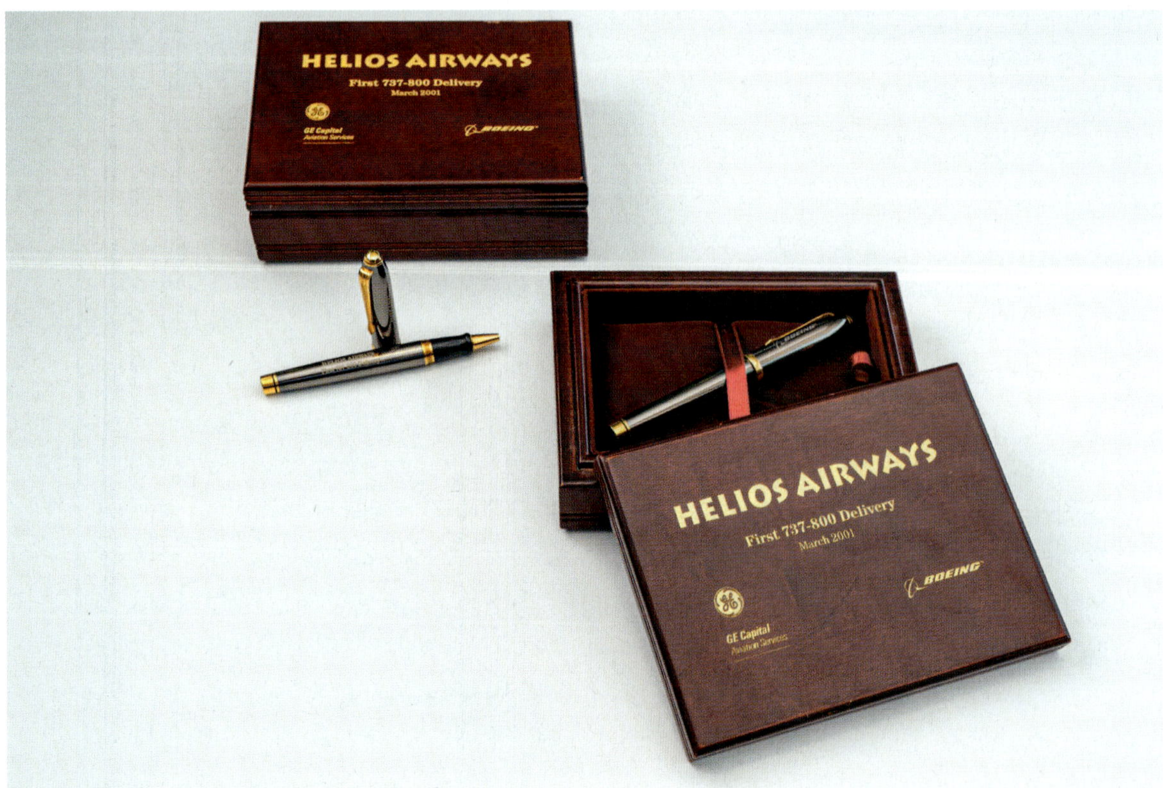

LEFT: A commemorative pen was given to Andreas Christodoulides following the handover of the carrier's two brand new Boeing 737-800s in early 2001

aircraft provide state-of-the-art operations and a heightened level of comfort. We are confident they will be perfect for our operations and popular with passengers."

From the outset, the Helios team had wanted to offer high levels of service on board. Fitted with 189 leather seats, the Next Generation 737s allowed them to do just that, with in-flight entertainment and complimentary meals and drinks – even serving passengers Starbucks coffee followed by the traditional Cypriot orange liqueur, Filfar.

On schedule

The arrival of the new jets coincided with the launch of Helios' new scheduled flights. At the time, the Cypriot government's bid to join the EU was gathering pace. As part of the requirements, it further liberalised its aviation policies by granting several scheduled route licences.

Helios, which had wanted to move into this market for some time, was granted scheduled rights to Belfast, Dublin and Sofia. Eurocypria was given the rights to fly to Rhodes. Meanwhile, a third licence was issued to Aerotrans Airlines, a Larnaca-based charter carrier that operated a single BAC One-Eleven, although details of this were not released.

On April 5, 2001, Helios' first scheduled service departed Larnaca, bound for Sofia, operated by Bravo Hotel. Christodoulides explained that the routes had been chosen after "identifying a gap in the market to destinations where Cyprus Airways didn't fly." The route proved so popular that it continued through the winter 2001/2002 timetable.

In March 2002, Helios launched its second scheduled route: a direct, twice-weekly rotation to Dublin, becoming the only Cypriot airline to fly to the Irish capital. As with Sofia, the route proved popular with tour operators block-booking seats. Further bilateral agreements between the UK and Cyprus allowed Helios to introduce daily   »

Seattle site on March 20, 2001, before being flown to its new home in Larnaca. It was followed shortly after by sister ship 5B-DBI (c/n 30807) *Veni*, which was flown to London/Luton to be presented to the media, tour operators and travel agents from the UK, the airline's biggest market. This was followed by a celebratory flight over the capital.

Speaking at the time, Christodoulides remarked: "The arrival of the second modern 737-800 achieves our short-term target. Both

BELOW: Helios' philosophy was "to operate a profitable low cost airline that will provide to its passengers the maximum possible safety, highest levels of service and competitive fares"

scheduled services to London/Luton in December 2002, catering to the large Cypriot community in North London.

The three scheduled links continued to operate successfully alongside Helios' growing charter market, which had expanded to serve several tour operators, as well as ad-hoc charter flights for special interest and private groups. The introduction of scheduled services saw the airline launch Helios Plus, a premium service that afforded passengers priority check-in, lounge access, 30kg of luggage allowance and seating in the Helios Plus cabin.

Additional scheduled route licences were applied for from both Larnaca and Paphos to

ABOVE: The arrival of the 737-800s allowed the airline to commence scheduled operations, initially to Sofia and Dublin

destinations including Alexandria, Manchester, Birmingham, Glasgow, Newcastle and Tel Aviv. The airline had previously applied for charter rights to operate to Tel Aviv from Paphos when it first commenced operations, but the application was rejected, with no reason given for the decision.

In April 2004, Helios also introduced a six-year-old ex-Deutsche BA Boeing 737-300, 5B-DBY (c/n 29099) *Olympia*, with 136 seats to complement its fleet. The airline had planned to add a third 737-800, but as there were none available at the time, the decision was made to add the smaller -300.

On May 1, 2004, Cyprus finally became a full member of the European Union. On the same day,

ABOVE: The airline's in-flight magazine, *Sunrays*

Helios launched a new five-times weekly service to London/Heathrow, in direct competition with Cyprus Airways and British Airways.

Twice-daily flights to Athens and Thessaloniki began on May 6, operated under a new codeshare agreement with Aegean Airlines.

Sale to Libra Holidays

However, Helios' arrival onto these key routes caused a stir with Olympic and Cyprus Airways, as Christodoulides observed: "They hit us hard by lowering their prices, which made the Athens and Thessaloniki routes financially unstable."

The airline's profits were impacted and in, October 2004, Christodoulides decided to sell the company: "I was commuting between London and Larnaca all the time and I wanted to spend more time with my family. I had a few offers on the table, including one from Cyprus Airways, but I believed they would close Helios down and people would lose their jobs. So we sold it a month later to Libra Holidays, a UK tour operator owned by Greek Cypriots, which we believed would bring expansion to the airline and to the tourism of Cyprus."

After the £2.4m deal, in December 2004, founder Andreas Christodoulides departed the company to focus on his shipping business, describing his departure as "a sad day, especially as the company was my baby."

Libra Holidays was a UK-based tour operator which had recently sold its 30% stake in Excel Airways to the Icelandic group Avion. The acquisition of Helios allowed it to expand into the scheduled flight market and strengthen its position in Cyprus.

Beginning of the end

Following the Libra takeover, issues began to arise. Several routes continued to underperform, including the Athens service. The airline's coveted Heathrow operation also had problems. Helios had been given a slot into the busy »

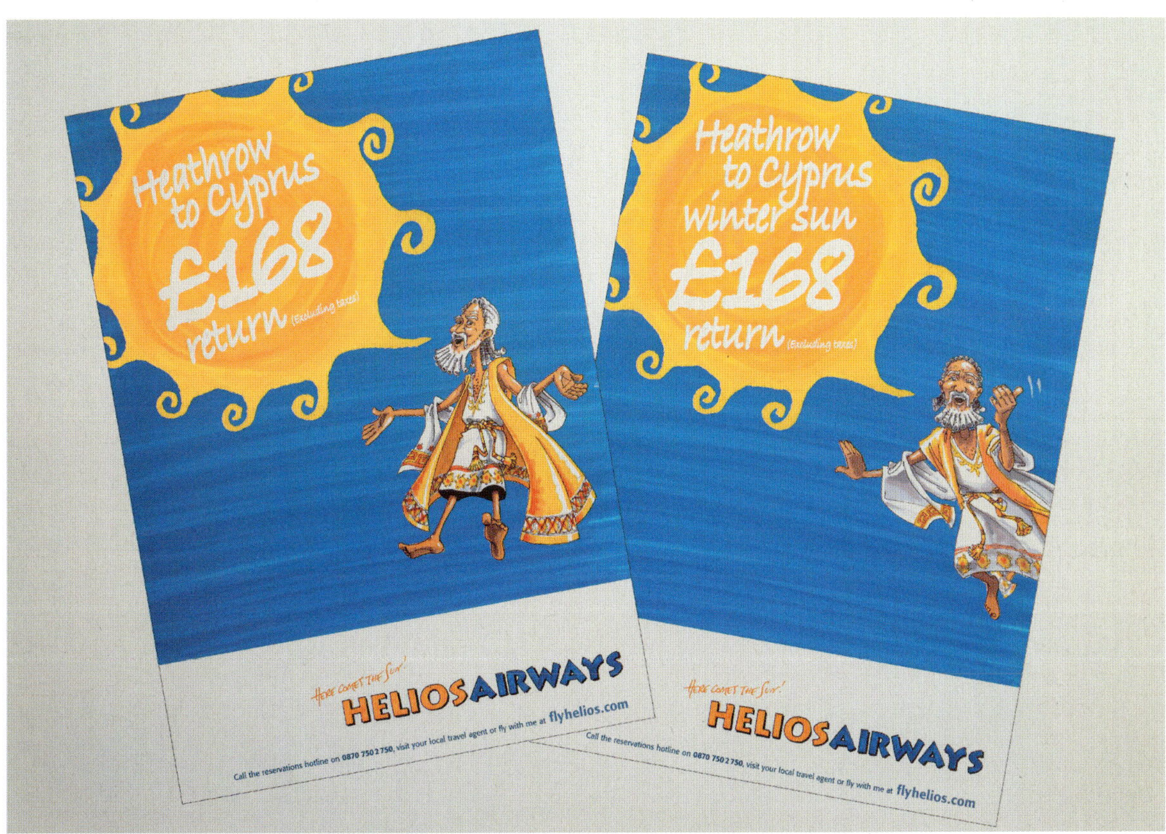

RIGHT: In a significant coup for the airline, on May 1, 2004, a new direct scheduled service to London/Heathrow was launched, coinciding with Cyprus joining the European Union

London hub late in the evening, which sometimes meant that the aircraft missed the airport's curfew and was forced to divert to Luton, which badly affected the company's reputation. Meanwhile, underperforming routes such as Paphos to Birmingham and London/Stansted were slashed from the network.

Then, on August 14, 2005, Helios Airways suffered the tragic loss of Flight 522, which profoundly affected the company's operations and reputation (see *Helios Flight 522*). In the wake of the disaster, Libra Holidays announced that all Helios operations would transition to a new carrier – ajet Airways – which was formally registered on January 20, 2006. By March that year, the Helios name was gone, along with the airline's former scheduled route network, as the company chose to focus exclusively on charter operations. Just eight months later, management announced that ajet would cease all operations from November 6, with most of its flights taken over by UK charter carrier XL Airways.

When the Helios name disappeared from the skies, many remembered it for the crash of Flight 522. But its legacy went way beyond that and remains an important part of European aviation history. As Cyprus' first private airline, it revolutionised travel to and from the island by breaking the long-standing monopoly in the country's commercial aviation market, lowering fares, making air travel more affordable and attracting new visitors. **AC**

ABOVE: A selection of Helios timetables and brochures, highlighting the carrier's clever and colourful marketing

BELOW: Following the crash of Helios Flight 522, the airline was rebranded as ajet by its new owners, Libra Holidays. Both of Helios' 737-800s were transferred over to the new carrier and joined by a third example, 5B-DCE (c/n 33029) AIRTEAMIMAGES.COM/ SIMON WILSON

Helios Airways fleet list						
Registration	Type	C/n	Name	First flight	Delivered	Notes
5B-DBG	Boeing 737-4Y0	24682	Athena	15/2/1990	17/5/2000	To Malév Hungarian Airlines
5B-DBH	Boeing 737-86N	30806	Zela	23/2/2001	20/3/2001	To Ajet
5B-DBI	Boeing 737-86N	30807	Veni	11/4/2001	25/4/2001	To Ajet
5B-DBY	Boeing 737-31S	29099	Olympia	29/12/1997	16/4/2004	Written off

Helios Flight 522

On August 14, 2005, a Helios Airways Boeing 737-31S, 5B-DBY (c/n 29099) *Olympia*, operating flight ZU522, a scheduled service from Larnaca to Prague with a stopover in Athens, crashed near the village of Grammatiko in a rural area of Greece, just outside of Athens. All 115 passengers, including Greek, Cypriot and Australian nationals, plus six crew members, were killed. It remains the worst air disaster in Greek aviation history.

The night before the crash, the 737 had flown in from London and, during this sector, the crew had reported issues with the right aft starboard service door. Writing in the aircraft's tech log, the crew said that the seal around the door had frozen and hard bangs had been heard during the flight. That evening, a pressure check was carried out in Larnaca by a Helios engineer and the jet was deemed serviceable for the flight to Prague the following day.

In charge of ZU522 was Captain Hans-Jürgen Merten. The 59-year-old German had previously flown for East German airline Interflug and UK low-cost carrier easyJet, accruing more than 16,900 flight hours, 5,500 of which had been on the 737. He was assisted by First Officer Pampos Charalambous, a 51-year-old Cypriot, who had worked for Helios for five years, amassing 7,549 hours, nearly 4,000 of which were on the 737. They were joined by four cabin crew.

Just over five minutes after take-off, the cabin altitude warning alarm began to sound on the flight deck as they passed through 12,000ft. Confused, the flight crew believed that the alarm was a take-off configuration warning – the alert sound was identical for both – and continued the climb. Then various other alarms began to sound, including the master caution and passenger oxygen lights at an altitude of around 16,000ft. At 18,000ft, the oxygen masks in the cabin automatically deployed.

Captain Merten radioed the airline's operations centre and reported "The take-off configuration warning on" and "Cooling equipment normal and alternate offline." Merten then spoke to the engineer who had conducted the pressurisation leak check, who asked if the pressurisation panel had been set to 'AUTO'.

By now, the symptoms of hypoxia were beginning to set in. As the 737 climbed through 28,900ft, Captain Merten asked: "Where are my equipment cooling circuit breakers?" The engineer on the ground replied: "Behind the captain's seat." This was the final communication before both pilots fell unconscious. The Cockpit Voice Recorder (CVR) led investigators to believe that the captain had got out of his seat to check the circuit breakers, but was overcome by the lack of oxygen. With the aircraft's autopilot set, the 737 continued its climb towards Athens, levelling off at 34,000ft. Nicosia ATC repeatedly attempted to contact the stricken jet, but there was no reply.

At 1040hrs, Flight 522 entered the holding pattern for Athens and remained there for the next 70 minutes, flying in a loop over the Greek capital. Continued attempts to contact the ghost plane remained unanswered. It was at this point that the Hellenic Air Force dispatched two F-16 fighter jets to establish visual contact with the 737, which they achieved at 1124hrs as the aircraft was entering its sixth loop of the holding pattern.

The pilots reported that they could see the first officer slumped motionlessly at the controls, but the captain's seat was empty. While the cabin was reportedly in darkness, they observed that the passenger oxygen masks, which last only for 12 minutes, had been deployed and three passengers were seen sat motionless, wearing their masks.

At 0849hrs, one of the air force pilots witnessed a person, whom they believed was not wearing an oxygen mask, entering the flight deck and taking the captain's seat. This was backed up by data recovered from the CVR, which revealed sounds matching someone using the flight deck door access code and the door opening. They put on a set of headphones and seemed to place their hands directly on the panel in front of them. The fighter pilot attempted to attract their attention, but to no avail. DNA tests later revealed that this was cabin crew member Andreas Prodromou, who held a pilot's licence but was not qualified to fly a 737.

A minute later, the left engine flamed out due to fuel exhaustion and the jet began to descend. Prodromou then sent two desperate distress messages, picked up on the CVR: "Mayday, Mayday, Mayday, Helios Airways Flight 522 Athens (unintelligible word)". A few seconds later, another "Mayday, Mayday" was recorded.

As the 737 descended through 7,000ft, Prodromou finally appeared to acknowledge the presence of the F-16s, making a hand motion. The pilot of the fighter jet responded with a hand signal for the person to follow him down towards the airport. Prodromou pointed downwards, but did not follow. Instead, at 0859hrs, the aircraft's heading changed to a southwesterly direction. This is believed to have been Prodromou's heroic last effort to guide the stricken airliner away from the Greek capital. The F-16 pilot also later reported that the way in which the 737 impacted the ground appeared to indicate that Prodromou attempted to level the wings to alleviate the impact. The right-hand engine flamed out as the aircraft descended through 7,000ft, before continuing a rapid descent and impacting hilly terrain near Grammatiko village, around 33km northwest of Athens, at 0903hrs.

The subsequent investigation by the Hellenic Air Accident Investigation and Aviation Safety Board (AAISB) revealed that the engineer carrying out the check on the rear aft service door had failed to reset a crucial air conditioning switch from 'MANUAL' to 'AUTO' after pressurising the aircraft. The pilots subsequently missed this error during their pre-departure checks and, as the Boeing jet climbed out of Larnaca, the cabin failed to pressurise.

The incident also highlighted issues regarding the locking of flight deck doors, introduced following the 9/11 terrorist attacks. At the time, only the senior cabin crew member was given the emergency access code for the door. Since training on emergency procedures for the door was relatively new, questions were raised about the crew's awareness of these new policies.

The Boeing 737-31S involved in the crash, 5B-DBY (c/n 29099) *Olympia*, was just six years old when it was delivered to Helios Airways, after previously flying for Deutsche BA AIRTEAMIMAGES.COM/ISMAEL JORDA

The jet crashed near the village of Grammatiko, just outside of Athens. All 115 passengers, plus six crew members, were killed. It remains the worst air disaster in Greek aviation history ALAMY/ASSOCIATED PRESS

"Island in Sight: Straight in to Land"

ON A MOONLESS NIGHT IN JULY 1950, A BOAC ARGONAUT SUFFERED ENGINE FAILURE MIDWAY ACROSS THE SOUTH ATLANTIC. DAVID RANSTED RECALLS A TALE OF COURAGE AND AIRMANSHIP THAT AVERTED DISASTER

British Overseas Airways Corporation (BOAC) flight BA371/184 was a scheduled service from London to Rio de Janeiro via Lisbon, Dakar and Natal. Late on July 20, 1950 it departed the Senegalese capital for Brazil, operated by Canadair C-4 Argonaut, G-ALHN (c/n 160) *Argosy*, and carrying a crew of seven along with 12 passengers plus one dog. Under the command of Captain R C 'Cliff' Alabaster, the aircraft's path took it over the South Atlantic into a dark, moonless night in calm weather above gentle seas.

BOAC had inherited the routes to South America after its 1949 merger with British South American Airways (BSAA) and most of the crews on the South Atlantic run had been with the latter — headed up by Air Vice-Marshal Don Bennett, who led the RAF's Pathfinder Force for much of World War Two. He personally selected

```
COPY


BOA MBK DE BOA LAP 169/21 =

DAKAR 210325 =

MAJOR DEFECT +

MEADOWBANK =

MEADOWBANK LAP LONDON BRENTFORD

IMMEDIATE AIRCRAFT SOS GALHN AT 0300 NR 3 NO3

FEATHERED NO 4 ENGINE ON FIRE DESCENDING 0220N 2725W

FULL DISTRESS PROCEEDURE IN OPERATION

0424 VH.
```

RIGHT: First Officer Derek Harry Shorter served in the RAF from August 1941 to December 1946 and flew Wellington, Lincoln, Halifax and Lancaster aircraft

FAR RIGHT: Navigation Officer Alfred Arthur Pearce's navigation skills were fully exercised on BOAC's Argonauts, covering a wide range BOAC's network, including Africa, the Americas and the Far East

LEFT: The airline's London Airport base received first news of the unfolding incident via telegram in the early hours of July 21, 1950

BELOW: BOAC Canadair C-4 Argonaut, G-ALHN (c/n 160) *Argosy* was delivered new to the airline on August 23, 1949, the twelfth out of 22 ordered by the corporation ALL IMAGES BA HERITAGE CENTRE UNLESS STATED

many BSAA crew from among the ranks of Bomber Command, including Captain Alabaster.

Although originally ordered for its routes to the east, BOAC rostered Argonauts onto its Brazilian services following the grounding of its ill-fated Avro Tudors after a series of incidents.

Point of no return

For almost four hours after the 2229hrs (GMT) departure, the crossing had been uneventful, cruising through the darkness at 20,000ft (6,096m) above the Atlantic – Argosy's four Rolls-Royce Merlin engines running off the auxiliary fuel tanks at a steady 2,520rpm.

Regular in-flight instrument checks showed nothing untoward, but just after switching flight watch control from Dakar to Natal radio at 0220hrs (GMT), around 30 minutes beyond the point of no return calculated on the flight plan, the sound of the engine changed to a high-pitched whine.

The instrument panel indicated an overspeed and Captain Alabaster ordered First Officer Shorter to

feather No.4 engine – to align the propeller blades to minimise air resistance – while Radio Officer Tanner sent an immediate 'XXX' signal (one level below SOS) to Natal asking them to stand by.

Shortly afterwards, the sound of the engine returned to normal and Alabaster concluded it had been a 'runaway' (when an engine draws additional fuel from an unintended source) resulting in overspeed to 3,500rpm.

Any relief in the cockpit was shortlived however, as the high-pitched whine returned a »

The Crew

Captain:	R C Alabaster
First Officer:	D H Shorter
Navigation Officer:	A Pearce
Radio Officer:	H J Tanner
Steward:	A T Lemon
Steward:	M J Lowe
Stewardess:	R S March

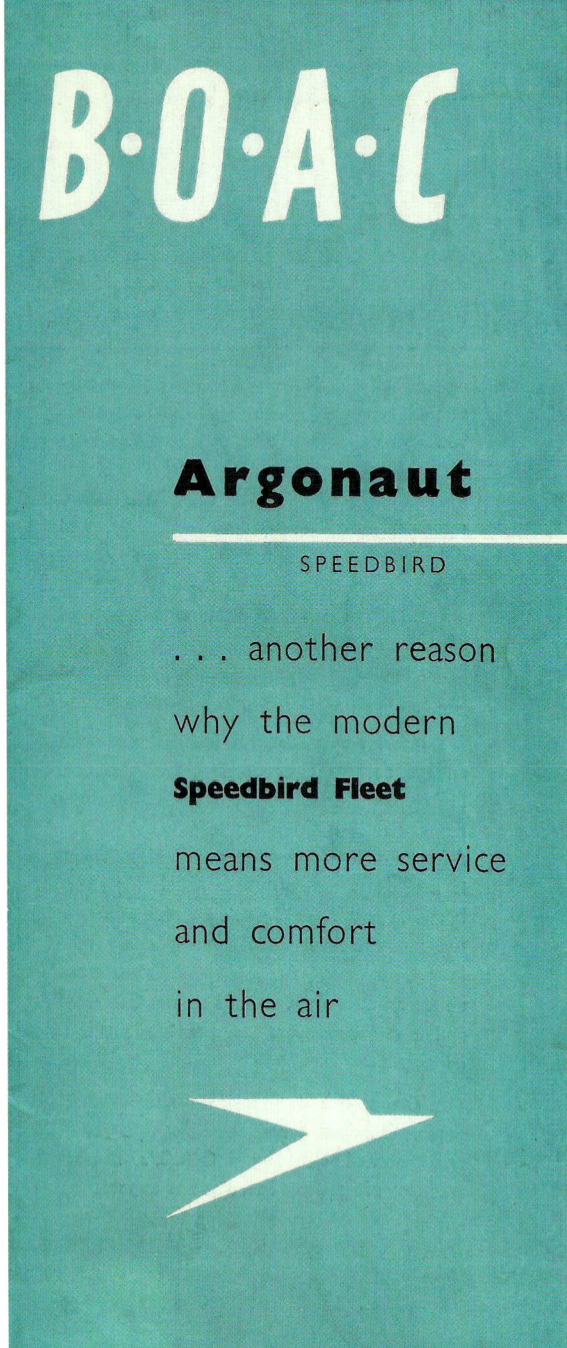

LEFT: Captain Alabaster, known as 'All-Bee' to his friends, flew for the carrier from 1949 until 1973

At 0230hrs, the altitude was down to 11,500ft, Argosy losing height at a rate of 400 feet per minute. With reduced height and speed, and two engines shut down – one with a propeller causing drag – the crew realised they may not reach the South American coast.

Quickly weighing up their options, at 0240hrs Tanner informed Natal of Argosy's situation and their decision to head for the tiny archipelago of Fernando de Noronha – the nearest landfall – 480 miles (772km) to the southwest. From this point on, he issued frequent position updates by Morse code to Natal and by radiotelephony to Dakar.

The control room in the Senegalese capital informed a nearby BOAC Avro York, G-AGNY (c/n 1226) – its crew altering course to follow Argosy's track – while a Panair Constellation, flying the opposite route from Natal to Dakar, was told the Argonaut's position and asked to keep a lookout. Natal also informed the crew of the Argonaut that the Brazilian Air Force base on Fernando de Noronha was on standby and in a position to help.

Alabaster switched from auxiliary to main tanks and increased power on No.1 and No.2 engines to 2,850rpm to arrest the descent. The No.3 oil tank contents gauge registered zero and its rpm indicator was not functioning. Unable to restart the engine, he lowered the airspeed to 120kts to reduce not only the risk of fire returning, but also potential overspeeding.

Establishing contact with Fernando de Noronha, the crew noted weather conditions and obtained position reports, and Argosy soon 'homed' on the airfield's beacon.

They then settled down to assess their situation. The No.2 engine coolant warning light was on almost continuously and No.1's began flickering as the coolant temperature crept above 140°C due to overheating at 11,000ft. The crew discussed trying to restart No.4 in the knowledge that there were no more extinguisher bottles in the starboard wing should the fire return.

As there had been no visible flames in No.4, and there was enough oil to re-feather if required, they attempted a restart – and the rpm slowly increased. The engine behaved normally and the

LEFT: The Argonauts were a step up in comfort for passengers compared to the Avro Yorks and Lancastrians they replaced and BOAC eagerly promoted

BELOW: The Argonaut was configured in a 2x2 layout

minute later and Shorter saw white flames from both sides of the No.3 Merlin – and the crew began the procedure for an engine fire.

Not only had it oversped to 4,000rpm, the crew soon discovered its oil pressure and contents gauges were reading zero and the engine had stopped running. Argosy quickly lost height and speed – and by 0225hrs it was flying at 13,000ft and 140kts.

Alabaster ordered the transmission of an SOS giving their position, along with course and speed, which was acknowledged by both Natal and Dakar. The first shot from the extinguisher bottles had doused the flames on the outside of the engine but it continued to burn on the inside, close to the exhaust stubs.

As the fire developed, the crew fired a second shot, but their relief that it had extinguished the flames soon turned to alarm when they realised the engine would not feather, causing significant drag and ultimately affecting the aircraft's range.

crew brought back the rpm on No.1 and No.2 to cruise level for 9,000ft.

Setting a lower power setting on No.2 to conserve coolant by keeping the temperature down, Argosy's crew faced a three-hour stretch over the empty ocean, with the port engines' coolant warning lights a constant cause for concern.

The drop in altitude finally halted at 9,000ft (2,743m) and the crew depressurised the aircraft and prepared everyone on board for ditching should the situation worsen.

Alabaster then calmly composed a signal outlining what had occurred so that, in the event of Argosy's loss, there would be a record of events.

In the passenger cabin, crew members A T Lemon, M J Lowe and R S March began the drill. They familiarised themselves with the release clips on the dinghy stowage harness and, where possible, the rafts were strapped down in seats alongside the escape positions to save time.

As an extra measure, each cabin crew member tied a torch to themselves to help keep the flashlight visible without having to use their hands. Lemon noted in his later report that the lifebelt container tabs were not secure enough and several ripped off when the containers were opened.

Needle in a haystack

The situation seemed to stabilise and the crew nursed the stricken Argonaut at reduced speed and altitude through the night sky, nervously monitoring the coolant warning lights of the port engines and peering out into blackness for a point of reference. They would need all their navigational skills, as astronavigation was impossible under the thick cloud cover.

The main island in the Fernando de Noronha archipelago is just six miles (10km) long and, at most, two miles (3.5km) wide. If the crew missed the tiny airstrip in the moonless night it would be another 220 miles (354km) to the Brazilian mainland.

Finally, at 0421hrs, two hours after the initial emergency, Argosy's navigator, A Pearce,

ABOVE: A map of Argosy's planned routing from London to Rio de Janeiro over the South Atlantic

established they were exactly on course and the flight proceeded steadily at its lower speed and altitude, the three engines behaving normally despite higher temperatures on the port side.

In a cruel twist, the crew then faced a final hurdle on being told that the landing lights at Fernando were unserviceable and airfield personnel would set out paraffin flares to guide them in, with an additional light shining down the runway from the touchdown end.

At 0609hrs Tanner reported to Fernando, "Island in sight. Straight in to land", and at 0622hrs, just as the sun rose behind them, and four hours after their ordeal had begun, Argosy made a textbook emergency landing on Fernando de Noronha's runway. Although ill-equipped to deal with »

> *"With reduced height and speed, and two engines shut down – one with a propeller causing drag – the crew realised they may not reach the South American coast."*

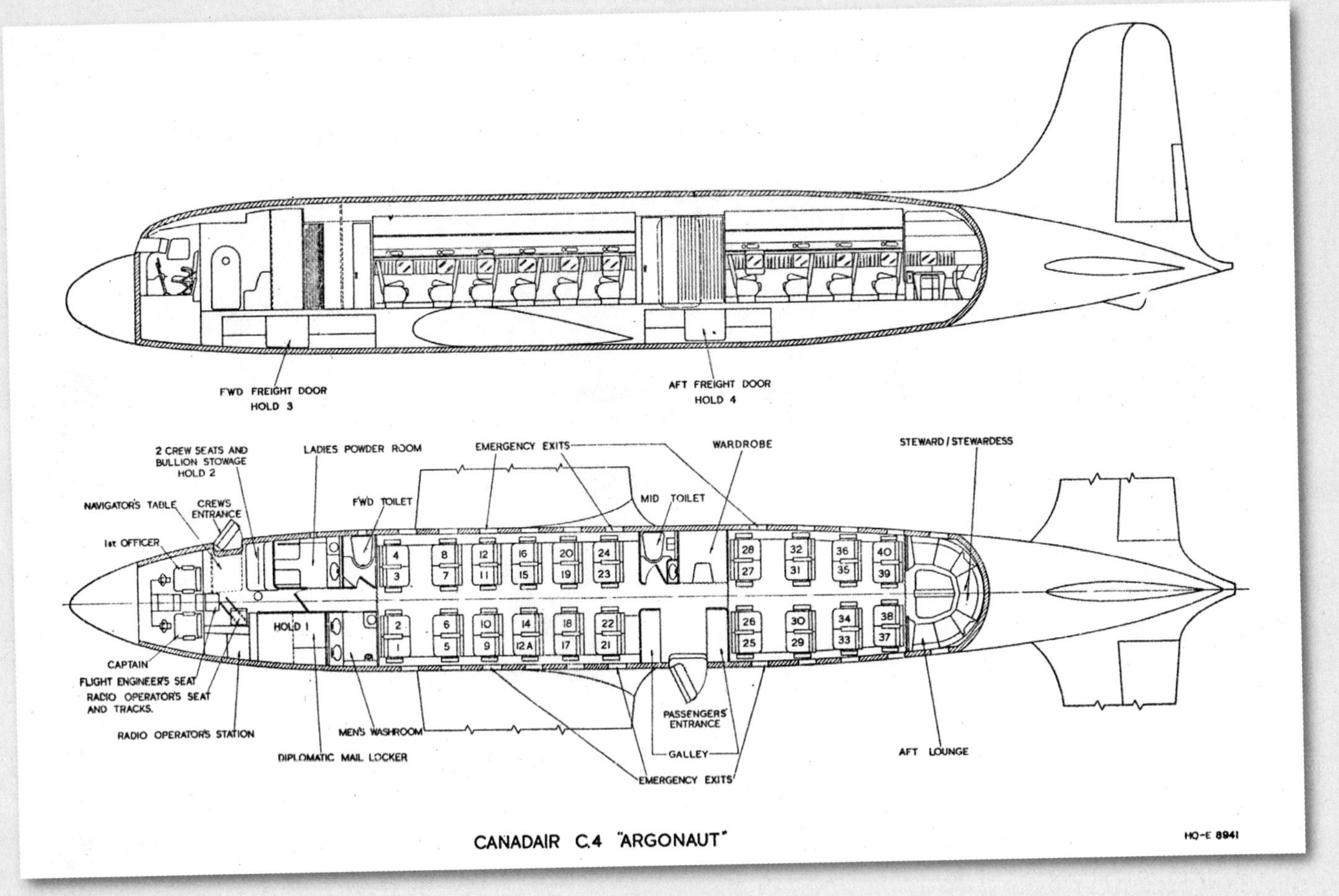

"In a cruel twist, the crew then faced a final hurdle on being told that the landing lights at Fernando were unserviceable"

civilians, the Brazilian Air Force personnel afforded the passengers and crew all the hospitality their rudimentary facilities allowed.

Fernando de Noronha

The main island of Fernando de Noronha's cluster of 12 in the South Atlantic, 220 miles (354km) off the northeast coast of Brazil, has an area of only 7.1 square miles (18.4km²). Opened in 1934, its airport was later expanded during World War Two by the US Army Air Force's Air Transport Command. In 2009 it served as a base for search and rescue operations following the crash of Air France 447, around 342 miles (550km) to the northeast. Today it's used by Brazilian commercial carriers Azul and GOL.

In his report Alabaster praised the conduct of the crew throughout the incident, saying they "did everything perfectly", and thanked the radio operators in Natal, Dakar and Fernando and the Brazilian Air Force.

The recovery

BOAC's Natal-based station engineer and traffic officer were dispatched to Fernando in a chartered PBY3 Catalina, joined by the route engineer and Lisbon station engineer. The flying boat carried the Argosy's passengers onwards to Natal while an Avro York freighter flew from London carrying a spare engine.   »

ABOVE: For the first part of their lives with BOAC, the Argonauts operated in an all-first class, two-cabin configuration, including a lounge at the rear

RIGHT: An extract from the flight's radio log shows the frequent communication between the crew of 'Argosy' and Natal as they coped with the emergency

BELOW: Although originally ordered for its routes to the east, BOAC rostered Argonauts onto its Brazilian services following the grounding of its ill-fated Avro Tudors

BRITISH OVERSEAS AIRWAYS CORPORATION

RADIO LOG EXTRACT

AIRCRAFT/CALL SIGN **G-ALHN** RADIO OFFICER **TANNER H.J.**
VOYAGE No. **571/184.** FROM **DAKAR** TO **NATAL** DATE **21/7/50.**

G.M.T.	TO	FROM	TX	RX	LOG
0206	ZWNT	GHN	6510	6510	QTC NR1/1 G-ALHN OPN 8 210201 = PPNT
					Starline = QAF 26 west 0200 QDP PPNT
					= G-HN
	G-HN	ZWNT	"	"	OK QDX PPNT
0208	G-HN	ZWNT	"	"	Natal 0200 QAN 140/10 QBA 20 knts. QBB
					4 SC 1200 QNH 1015.9 QNU 22/18
					E a c as 2000 = Meteo PPNT
	FOK	GHN	"	"	QTC NR3/1 G-ALHN OPN 8 210201 =
					FHDK Speedbird = QAF 26 west 0200
					QDX PPNT = G-HN.
0225	ZWNT	GHN	6510	6510	XXX QAP QTC as sec. (Runaway engine)
					SOS SOS SOS de G-ALHN (X3) at 0225 QTH
					0402N 2710W QTI 219 QTJ 240
			5105	5105	REPEATED.
					QSL s from ZWNT and FOK
					SOS (X3) G-ALHN (X3) at 0230 QTH
					0315N 2710W Nr. 4 engine feathered
					Nr. 3 on fire unable feather
0240					QTB FOK 221/2
0247	Radio				
	Natal		4220	4220	Rpt. SOS and say going to FN
		FOK			QTB 220
	ZWNT		6510		SOS de G-HN at 0300 0220 North
					2752 West QAH 9500 feet QTI 212
					Airspeed 145 on 2 engines.
	Radio				
	Natal	GHN	4220	4220	Rpt. on R/T = Fernando Noronha
					runway east 2135 metres long lights are
					--------(unable read) = QRX
	FOK	GHN			Inform G-AGNY
0310	GHN	FOK			219B QTB FOK
	Natal	GHN	4220		UPR 236 Kcs. on
	Natal	GHN	4220		At 0315 = Position 0419 North 2812 West
					8900 feet 212 degrees Airspeed 140
					E.T.A. Fernando 0600.
					SOS de GHN Repeat above
	GHN	ZWNT			QSL
	GHN	FOK			QSL
	GHN	FOK			Have informed GNY QAP
0334	GHN	ZWNT	6510		Nr. 2/1 ZWNT CTL 210330 = G-ALHN =
					Fernando Noronha on alert airforce notified
					for any action = PPNT Starline
0336	ZWNT	GHN			XXX XXX XXX at 0330 QTH 0120 North
					2635 West QAH 9000 feet QTI 212 Airspeed
					140 kts. on 2 engines QAB FN = GHN.
0340	ZWNT	GHN			Please despatch lifeboat carrier
					aircraft to meet us
	Radio	GHN	4220	4220	Repeat on R/T = Ses I will do.
	Natal				
		ZWNT	6510	6510	QRU? # Ere nil# QPS de FN
	ZWNT		6510		XXX XXX XXX at 0400 QTH 0032 North
0404	FOK				2919 West QAH 9000 feet QTI 209
					Airspeed 140 Kts. on 2 engines

At Fernando, the crew and engineers inspected Argosy and concluded that No.1 and No.2 engines were serviceable. No.3 engine's connecting rods had penetrated the side of the crankcase and the pitch angle of the propeller was such that the reduction gear casing gave way. As for No.4, no defects were found and it was considered serviceable.

After a ferry flight to Natal, the engines were checked again. No.1 and No.2 were deemed serviceable, but a replacement was required for No.3, which was described as "a complete wreck"; and while No.4 was largely in good shape, it was decided to change the CSU (constant speed unit) as part of further investigations to determine whether it had in fact 'run away'.

After installing new equipment, the aircraft behaved normally (with the engines now synchronised) on the ferry flight back to the UK on July 27, and even picked up passengers in Lisbon from a separate delayed service.

The investigation

In its findings, the Air Safety Committee concluded: "The Captain and First Officer are held not responsible for the incident. The entire crew are to be commended on their display of airmanship and team spirit throughout the emergency."

Both the committee and BOAC's internal inquiry concluded the incident was caused by the overspeed of No.3 and No.4 engines, and the failure of the former – but that, as a single revolution gauge was used for both engines, it was possible Alabaster may have erroneously feathered No.4 – a possibility he agreed with.

The report also said restarting it was correct, and feathering No.4 had not materially affected the handling of the crisis. The fire and failure of the third engine alone was sufficiently serious to warrant the emergency procedures and the decision to divert for an emergency landing.

No.4 engine had performed normally after the restart and later detailed investigation by BOAC engineers showed no signs of overspeeding – but also no conclusive proof that it hadn't oversped.

The failure of the No.3 engine was caused by serious and rapid oil depletion when a blanking plug came adrift, leading to main and connecting rod bearing seizure and engine overspeeding.

The investigation also concluded that the first fire extinguishing shot, at around 18,000ft and 150kts, had only reduced the flames because the fire had burned a hole through the engine casing through which the draught fanned the blaze. The second shot, fired at 15,000ft and 130kts, had succeeded in extinguishing the fire. The inquiry found that the behaviour of No.1 and No.2 engines had been "far below that advertised by the manufacturers and did not give assistance to the Captain when he was in urgent need".

'Ali-Bee'

Robert Clifford ('Cliff') Alabaster, DFC and Bar, DSO and Bar, known as 'Ali-Bee' to his friends, was a highly decorated war hero who flew on more than 100 raids with Bomber Command. Born on March 11, 1918 in Willesden, north London, he joined the RAF on May 1, 1938, rising to the rank of wing commander.

After the war he joined BSAA, going on to fly York, Lancastrian and Tudor aircraft. He

ABOVE: This BOAC Argonaut, G-ALHE (c/n 151) *Argo*, suffered a similar event to the South Atlantic incident, seen here in Entebbe on January 13, 1955 receiving attention for a suspected seized engine following a coolant leak. On this occasion, a camera was present to record it

ABOVE LEFT: BOAC operated a fleet of Canadair C-4 Argonauts from 1949 until 1960

LEFT: From props to jets, Captain 'Cliff' Alabaster in front of a BOAC Comet 4 GRAHAM PITCHFORK VIA THE AUTHOR

"Thanks to the skill, courage and determination of the crew, Argosy and her passengers were saved from near certain catastrophe..."

---

was navigation officer on board the very first scheduled departure from London Airport on January 1, 1946 – a BSAA Lancastrian service to Buenos Aires commanded by Don Bennett – and joined BOAC with the merger on August 1, 1949.

On May 2, 1952, Alabaster commanded the first commercial scheduled jet service over the Khartoum-Entebbe-Livingstone-Johannesburg sectors of BOAC's inaugural de Havilland Comet 1 service between London and Johannesburg, later commanding Comet 4 and Vickers VC10 types. Retiring from BOAC in 1973, he worked for British Caledonian and later flew VC10s for Gulf Air. He passed away in 2014 aged 95.

The report further noted the lack of ASR (air sea rescue) facilities in Senegal and Brazil, but acknowledged that all possible assistance had been given by Natal, Dakar and Fernando de Noronha. Many technical recommendations were also made following the incident, including several related to engine failure procedures, crew training and best practice for radio communications.

In his own summary, Alabaster made further suggestions, including separate rpm gauges for each engine and an established 'let-down' procedure for all alternate airfields.

Due recognition

Following the incident Alabaster, Shorter, Pearce and Tanner were each awarded BOAC's Certificate of Commendation for Exceptional Qualities of Leadership and Initiative, and Alabaster received the King's Commendation for Valuable Service in the Air.

It was later revealed that both Alabaster and Shorter had completed their latest survival and rescue instruction training on July 17, 1950 – just three days before the incident.

Argosy would continue to serve with BOAC until 1960, when it was sold to UK charter operator Overseas Aviation.

Thanks to the skill, courage and determination of the crew, Argosy and her passengers were saved from near certain catastrophe; yet despite this remarkable achievement, the incident remains little known among the general public to this day.

The author thanks Jim Davies and Keith Hayward of the British Airways Heritage Centre for their assistance in preparing this article. **A**

KLM's Fokker farewell

KLM'S 97-YEAR ASSOCIATION WITH DUTCH MANUFACTURER FOKKER CAME TO AN END WHEN IT RETIRED ITS LAST F70 IN OCTOBER 2017. THE DUTCH AIRLINE ENSURED IT WENT OUT IN STYLE, AS RICHARD SCHUURMAN REPORTS

Within eight minutes, they had all gone. First PH-KZU (c/n 11534), then PH-KZB (c/n 11562) and, after a brief pause, PH-KZL (c/n 11536) and PH-KZS (c/n 11540). The last four KLM Cityhopper Fokker 70s took off like rockets on their farewell flights from Amsterdam/Schiphol on October 29, 2017.

It ended an era in Dutch aviation, concluding a relationship between KLM and Fokker stretching back 97 years, despite a hiatus between 1940 and 1966.

The only one to return was 'KZU, proudly adorned with Anthony Fokker's portrait on its tailfin. Gear down, speed brakes open, it flew as slowly as possible over KLM Cityhopper's office at just 820ft (250m) for one final farewell, before joining the other three already en route to KLM UK Engineering in Norwich.

Observers could sense the emotion of the moment. The Fokkers' departure from the KLM Cityhopper fleet garnered newspaper coverage, television reports and even a book. The sombre mood was reminiscent of the

BELOW: KLM Cityhopper's Fokker 70s were a common sight at airports across the UK
KEY COLLECTION

ABOVE: The airline's first Fokker 70, PH-KZA (c/n 11567), wearing KLM Cityhopper's old livery, was delivered in February 1996 ALL PHOTOS KLM UNLESS STATED

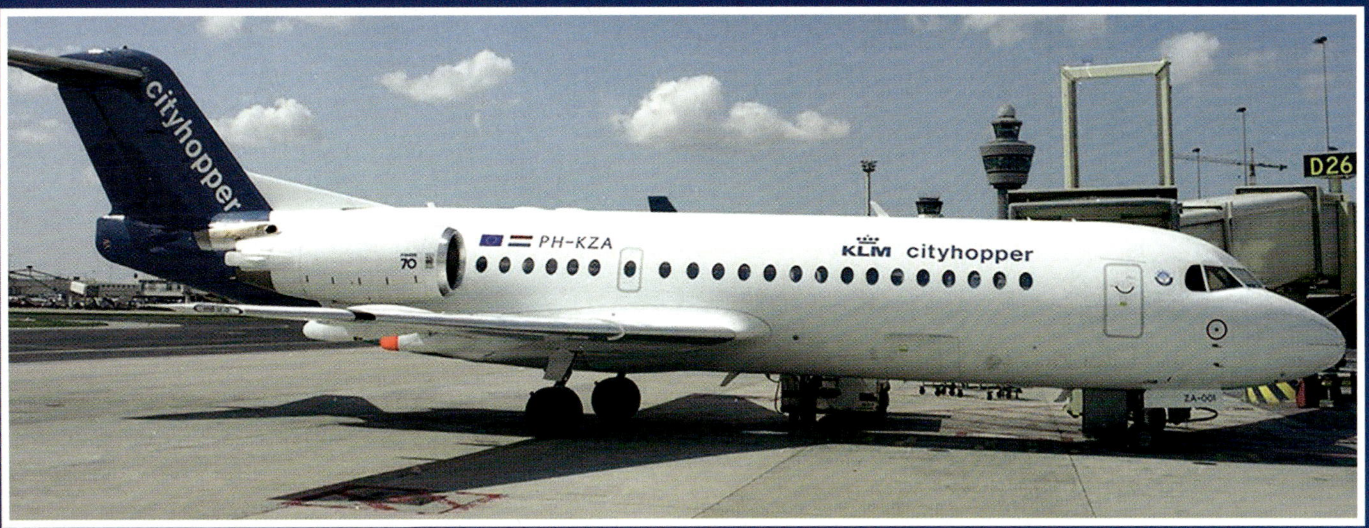

time Fokker went bankrupt in March 1996, ending the Netherlands' proud tradition of aircraft manufacturing. Now, some of the final aircraft to leave the company's production line were being disposed of by the country's national airline.

Planning

KLM had long planned for this moment. "The day Fokker went out of business, we already knew we had to replace the Fokkers in our fleet, even when at the time we had just started getting the first '70s", admitted former Cityhopper managing director Boet Kreiken, at the farewell event. "They are fine, well-built and robust aircraft, but without the support of a factory to develop them, it becomes very difficult to keep them flying. Who do you call when you need specific spare parts which might need to be recertified? That's when things started getting complex for an airline like ours, which wants to do six to seven rotations a day." »

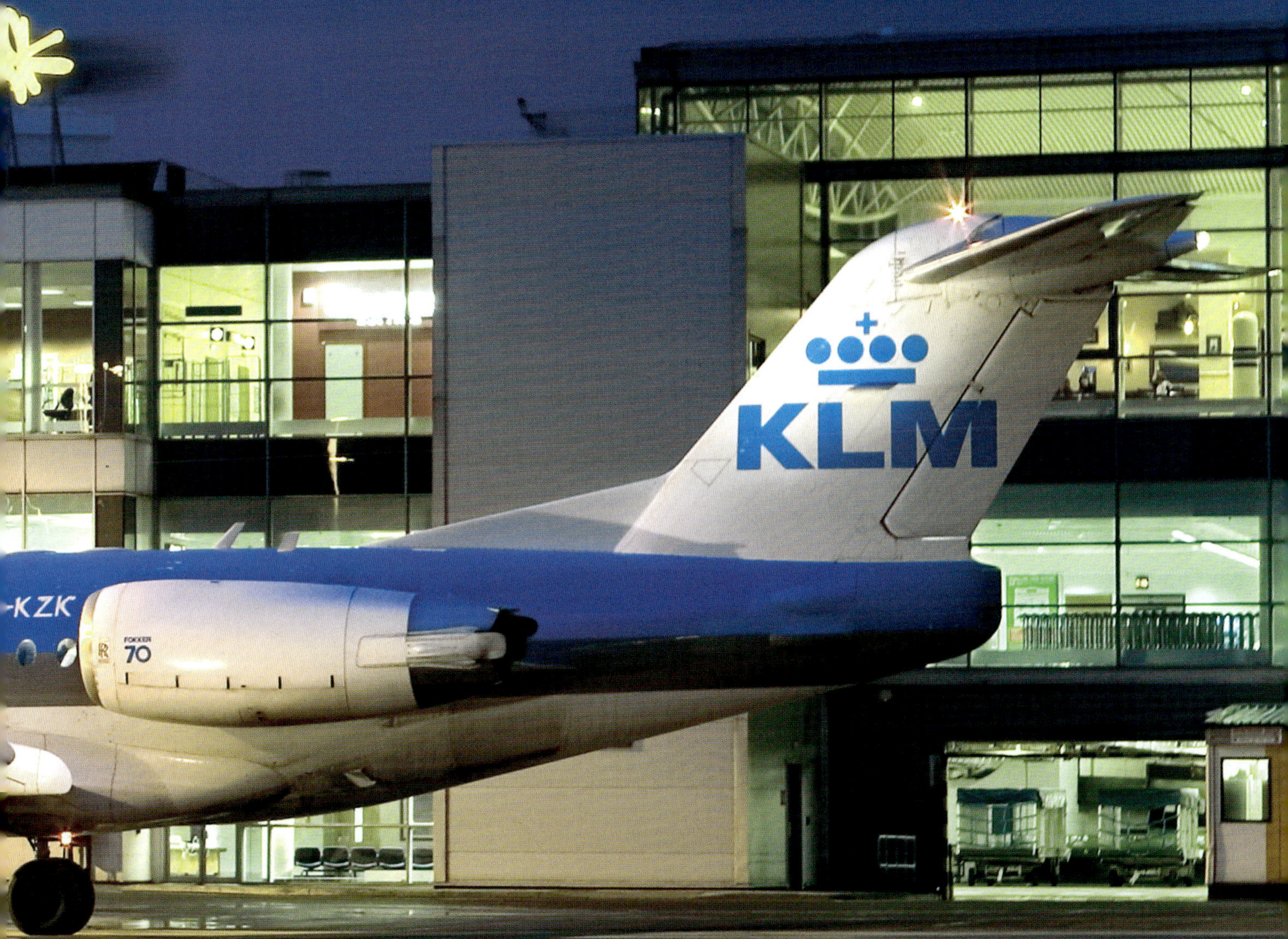

Kreiken said that meant the type was no longer viable for the carrier, although they were more than suitable for others.

Between 2010 and 2012, Cityhopper phased out its 22 F100s, replacing them with the Brazilian-built Embraer E190. In 2013, the airline ordered the smaller E175 to replace its 26 F70s. By the summer of 2018, Cityhopper planned to have 49 aircraft, making it the largest operator of the E-Jet in Europe.

"We operated the Embraers and Fokkers for nine years in parallel, which weighed heavy on the organisation because we had to do maintenance and crew training for both", explained KLM's former president and CEO Pieter Elbers. "It is always difficult to maintain reliability when the fleet size shrinks, so this is the right moment to bring forward some of the investments in Embraer. But saying farewell also hurts, the cosiness and familiarity of the Fokkers and a bit of Dutch pride has gone."

Little sister
Developed in 1992 as a smaller variant of the F100, the F70 is 101.4ft (30.9m) long, and although it looks identical to the F28, it is 4.2ft (1.3m) longer than the Fellowship.

ABOVE: 'Zulu Uniform' lifts off from Schiphol bound for Heathrow for the last time KLM/ ANDRES BOLKENBAAS

LEFT: Fokker veteran Waldo Berenschot described the F70 as a "pilot's aircraft"

BELOW: KLM Cityhopper commenced Fokker 70 operations in 1996. The airline would go on to become the type's biggest operator with 26 in the fleet at its peak, including PH-KZB (c/n 11562) seen departing Schiphol RICHARD SCHUURMAN

surface that you need to reach. Your inputs don't go through a computer or any fly-by-wire system, so you certainly feel the aircraft."

Galloway flew the F100 and F70 with Cityhopper, both briefly during the same period. "You can forget which one you are in, they are that similar", he explained. "With the '100, if you were landing and there was a little bit of turbulence, you could just give the control column a nudge and slide her onto the runway. On the '70 you can't play that trick as the wheels are closer to the centre of effort."

The F70 has the same Rolls-Royce Tay 620 engines available on the F100, which, to some, made it overpowered. "Some say underpowered, some say over", Galloway said. "She climbs very quickly for the initial part of the climb. I think it is about right."

Reliability

In the F70's last years of service with Austrian, the airline frequently experienced technical issues. KLM Cityhopper wasn't immune to similar problems, but former vice president Hans Werner praised the efforts of his airline and Nayak Aviation Services to keep the type flying. »

Only 48 airframes were built, of which Cityhopper got 26, Austrian Airlines 21 and the Dutch government one. PH-KZK (c/n 11581) was the last jet to leave the factory in April 1997 and was initially leased to Austrian.

Passengers liked the 80-seat F70, although not everyone was fond of the 2-3 cabin layout. The jet was also popular with cabin crew. "It was a very pleasant aircraft to work on, almost cosy, as she is relatively small", senior flight attendant Nicole van Rooijen said. "I worked on the Saab 340 and F50 before, and to me she was almost a big aircraft."

That affection extended to the cockpit as well. Waldo Berenschot flew every Fokker type during his 38-year career, describing the F70 as a "pilot's aircraft". "It is always very responsive to your input, not like a modern Airbus where you have a computer that decides", he explained. "You have to work hard in a Fokker."

Cityhopper Captain Richard Galloway agreed, "Once you have settled your seat in the correct position, you can reach every button and control

ABOVE: A monument, made from the tail of PH-KZW, was unveiled outside KLM Cityhopper's office at Schiphol to celebrate the airline's association with Fokker.

RIGHT: The aircraft could accommodate 80 passengers, seated in a 2-3 layout

BELOW: PH-KZG (c/n 11578) joined the Dutch carrier in October 1997, after having previously flown for Austrian Airlines. It was retired in February 2015 **KEY-TONY DIXON**

"Performance got better by the year, thanks to love and tender care from everyone involved", he said. "In her last year in service, we had the highest fleet availability ever since flying the Fokker 70. We went from 85% to 95% aircraft availability, while technical dispatch reliability went from 90% in 2008 to 97% this year." Despite the impressive increase in performance, Werner revealed Cityhopper's Embraer fleet boasted a 98% fleet availability at the time of the F70s retirement.

"It is only a 3% difference, but it means they can be used that bit more. They do seven rotations a day, while the Fokkers did five to six." Cityhopper aimed to further improve the reliability of its Embraer aircraft, so that in 2020, only one aircraft would be needed on standby compared with four Fokkers. The Brazilian-built jets provide benefits over the F70s in fuel costs too. Kreiken explained: "The E175 is 22% cheaper on fuel than the Fokker, as it has newer engines and more advanced aerodynamics.

"That made a huge difference when oil prices were at $110 a barrel, although the drop in fuel prices helped to extend the Fokker operations."

Phasing out

Once the decision to replace the F70s was made, the airline began phasing out the type. Werner explained: "We started planning all scheduled maintenance until the predicted last day in service. We looked at how much life there was left in each engine, gear and APU, as they are the most expensive parts. You don't want to have an expensive repair just before you retire the aircraft. We managed the fleet, selected the best parts and put them on the aircraft with the lowest number of flight hours. Basically, we exchanged parts from one aircraft to another, while at the same time using our inventories to the full." The first aircraft to leave the fleet was PH-KZV in January 2014, followed by 'KZG, 'JCH, 'WXA, 'KZW, 'JCT and 'KZH. The following year, 'KZF and 'KZN were retired and it was decided to bring the retirement of the last F70s forward from 2018 to October 2017 because of increasing maintenance costs. In 2016, 'KZO, 'WXC, 'KZT, 'KZR, 'KZA, and 'WXD departed, with 'KZD, 'KZE, 'KZC, and

ABOVE: The last four aircraft taxi out to the Oostbaan runway at Schiphol, nicknamed 'Fokkerbaan' due to the Fokker factory's proximity **KLM/ ANDRES BOLKENBAAS**

RIGHT: At the conclusion of flight KL1070, PH-KZU was given a traditional water cannon salute by the airport fire service

BELOW: All smiles: the cabin crew of flight KL1070 pose for more photos

'KZP following in October 2017. Most found new owners, with Papua New Guinea's Air Niugini taking eight and Aruba's InselAir four, while FlyAllways from Suriname and Air KBZ from Myanmar had two each. Two were disposed of: 'KZW was scrapped in 2015 after being stripped of all useful parts, and the same fate met 'KZT after a deal with InselAir fell through.

Final flights

When the last day of operations beckoned on October 28, there were only seven left. The fleet's record holder, 'KZL, with 45,434 flight hours before its last week in service, concluded its career with KLM the night before, when it returned from Humberside. Sistership 'KZK undertook its last flight to Brussels, returning to Amsterdam at 1900hrs, just ahead of 'KZB (Düsseldorf), 'KZM (Hannover), 'KZS (Norwich) and 'KZI (Luxembourg).

The last service, KL1070, landed at 2030hrs local time. The honour of performing this historic rotation was bestowed on 'KZU. Like the first-ever KLM Fokker flight, the destination was London. And while the F.II had gone to Croydon on September 30, 1920, the final flight used the city's modern gateway, Heathrow. »

"I worked on the very first Cityhopper Fokker 70 service in 1996 and now on the last one", said van Rooijen. "We had so many enthusiastic Fokker fans on board, only a few passengers weren't aware that this was the final one. All got a goodie bag and we served extra cake. The mood [on board] was all very cheerful."

From the front of the decorated cabin, filmed by almost 80 cameras, Captain Galloway addressed his passengers on the PA system, informing them that this was his last flight before retiring. "The company asked me to fly the very last flight of

ABOVE: The Fokker 70 played a pivotal role in the KLM Cityhopper fleet. Only 48 airframes were built, of which Cityhopper got 26, Austrian Airlines 21 and the Dutch government one

BELOW: In 2013, the airline ordered the smaller E175 to replace its 26 F70s

the Fokker, and what an enormous privilege that is. I have been the most senior British pilot at Cityhopper for over ten years now, and I flew the Fokker 100 and 70 variants for 25 years and 25 days. To be able to finish my career on this aeroplane with all this amazing publicity is absolutely lovely."

On departure from Heathrow, ATC wished the aircraft and Galloway farewell, while at Schiphol, ground vehicles escorted it to the ramp, where the passengers disembarked, before the jet continued to Hangar 73. There,

at the exact spot where Fokker assembled the aircraft, and Nayak and KLM had maintained them for 21 years, the fire service saluted 'KZU in front of staff and invited guests. At that same time, 'KZI and 'KZM were already on their way to Norwich, while 'KZK headed to Maastricht.

The next morning, a monument, created from the tail of 'KZW, was unveiled outside the airline's office at Schiphol, celebrating the partnership between KLM, Cityhopper and Fokker.

ABOVE: The honour of operating the final flight, KL1070 to London/Heathrow, was bestowed on 'KZU, resplendent in its Fokker-themed special livery, which made a final flypast at Schiphol before joining the other aircraft en route to Norwich
RICHARD SCHUURMAN

The last four aircraft then started up and took off from the Oostbaan runway, nicknamed 'Fokkerbaan' due to the factory's proximity, ready for their farewell flypast. As the jets disappeared out of sight, the curtain fell on KLM's 97-year association with Fokker.

"For all seven that have left now we have signed contracts, but we will only disclose the new owners once everything has been finalised", revealed Werner, adding only that they were destined for Peru, Panama, Afric, Cyprus and probably New Guinea. A

KLM Cityhopper Fokker 70 Fleet List

Reg	Type	C/n	Fleet number	Delivery date	Exit date	Notes
PH-KZA	Fokker 70 (F28-0070)	11567	ZA-001	7/2/1996	29/10/2016	To Air Niugini
PH-KZB	Fokker 70 (F28-0070)	11562	ZB-002	23/2/1996	20/10/2017	To Tus Airways
PH-KBX	Fokker 70 (F28-0070)	11547	N/A	12/3/1996	19/2/2017	Operated for Government of the Netherlands
PH-KZC	Fokker 70 (F28-0070)	11566	ZC-003	3/5/1996	3/7/2017	To Myamar Air Force
PH-KZE	Fokker 70 (F28-0070)	11576	ZE-005	4/10/1996	1/3/2017	To Myamar Air Force
PH-KZF	Fokker 70 (F28-0070)	11577	ZF-006	28/10/1996	24/10/2015	To Air Niugini
PH-KZD	Fokker 70 (F28-0070)	11582	ZD-004	22/1/1997	5/2/2017	To Air Niugini
PH-KZI	Fokker 70 (F28-0070)	11579	ZI-009	26/3/1997	28/10/2017	To Fly All Ways
PH-KZG	Fokker 70 (F28-0070)	11578	ZG-007	7/10/1997	3/2/2017	Ex-Austrian Airlines. To Air Niugini
PH-KZH	Fokker 70 (F28-0070)	11583	ZH-008	22/10/1997	26/5/2014	Ex-Austrian Airlines. To Insel Air
PH-KZK	Fokker 70 (F28-0070)	11581	ZK-010	3/11/1997	28/10/2017	Ex-Austrian Airlines. To Jetways Airlines
PH-WXA	Fokker 70 (F28-0070)	11570	XA-011	15/12/1997	30/3/2014	To Fly All Ways
PH-WXC	Fokker 70 (F28-0070)	11574	XC-012	15/12/1997	25/3/2016	To Air Niugini
PH-KZM	Fokker 70 (F28-0070)	11561	ZM-014	31/5/2000	28/10/2017	Ex-SilkAir. To Tus Airways
PH-KZN	Fokker 70 (F28-0070)	11553	ZN-015	27/9/2001	28/12/2015	Ex-Pelita Air Service. To Insel Air Aruba
PH-KZO	Fokker 70 (F28-0070)	11538	ZO-018	29/3/2002	1/4/2016	Ex-bmi British Midland. To Air Niugini
PH-KZR	Fokker 70 (F28-0070)	11551	ZR-020	16/4/2002	9/3/2016	Ex-bmi British Midland. To Air Niugini
PH-JCH	Fokker 70 (F28-0070)	11528	CH-016	10/4/2002	3/3/2014	To Insel Air
PH-KZP	Fokker 70 (F28-0070)	11539	ZP-019	10/4/2002	10/2/2017	Ex-bmi British Midland. To Wayraperú
PH-JCT	Fokker 70 (F28-0070)	11537	CT-017	25/10/2002	5/12/2014	To Insel Air
PH-WXD	Fokker 70 (F28-0070)	11563	XD-021	18/11/2004	29/10/2016	To Air Niugini
PH-KZW	Fokker 70 (F28-0070)	11558	ZW-026	27/10/2008	30/4/2014	Tail fin preserved at AMS
PH-KZT	Fokker 70 (F28-0070)	11541	ZT-023	5/2/2009	1/5/2016	Scrapped in 2016
PH-KZU	Fokker 70 (F28-0070)	11543	ZU-024	3/4/2009	28/10/2017	Painted in "Anthony Fokker (Farewell) livery. To Tus Airways
PH-KZV	Fokker 70 (F28-0070)	11556	ZV-025	10/9/2009	5/1/2014	To Fly All Ways
PH-KZS	Fokker 70 (F28-0070)	11540	ZS-022	7/10/2009	28/10/2017	To Wayraperú

The aircraft that shrank the world

BOB O'BRIEN CHARTS THE EARLY DAYS OF THE BOEING 747 AND ITS ENTRY INTO SERVICE WITH BRITAIN'S BOAC, WHICH TAILORED ITS NEW JUMBO JET TO OFFER PASSENGERS THE VERY FINEST ONBOARD EXPERIENCE

Legend has it that two aviation heavyweights, William 'Bill' McPherson Allen, president of the Boeing Airplane Company, and Juan Terry Trippe, founder of Pan American World Airways, were fishing one summer day in Puget Sound, Washington State, when the conversation turned to the need for an advanced jet aircraft. The airliner had to be bigger and better than anything that had come before it and be capable of travelling vast distances at a profit to whoever would take such a gamble on the new jet.

As the two friends fished, Trippe asked Allen: "Would you build it if I bought it?" Allen replied: "Would you buy it if I built it?" And so the seeds

BELOW: The prototype Boeing 747, N7470 (c/n 20235), was rolled out of the factory in Everett on September 30, 1968, to much fanfare KEY COLLECTION

RIGHT: Boeing 747-126, G-AWNF (c/n 19766), had the honour of operating BOAC's inaugural jumbo jet flight on April 14, 1971, which departed at 1203hrs bound for New York/JFK ALL IMAGES BOB O'BRIEN COLLECTION UNLESS STATED

were sown for what was to become a legend in its lifetime: the Boeing 747.

By the mid-1960s, the early jets on the North Atlantic routes were showing signs of being unable to cope with market growth. The major US aircraft manufacturers took note and started to think big about designing the next generation of passenger transport. Boeing, Douglas and Lockheed participated in a USAF competition to design a large transport aircraft that would be twice the size of anything that had taken to the skies before. Lockheed won with a design called the C-5A Galaxy.

Although the Galaxy was a huge success for the USAF, it was deemed unsuitable for carrying passengers over long distances. Undeterred, Boeing's designers used the knowledge gained from the military project to develop a concept that would serve the airlines of the world for years to come.

Design and development

One of the initial plans for the Boeing 747 featured a mid-wing design and a double-decker fuselage with a width much greater than its stablemate, the 707. Boeing advertised the aircraft to airlines worldwide as ushering in a new era in transportation, with twin-aisle comfort and an upstairs lounge that could be used as a bar for first-class customers, accessed by a spiral staircase adjacent to door 1 left. Its other dimensions were equally impressive, with a wingspan of 59.64m, a length of 70.51m and a maximum take-off weight of 378,000kg.

Power was to be provided by Pratt & Whitney, with an engine that would give more thrust than anything they had provided before, the JT9D turbofan. The JT9D would provide 43,500lb of thrust and a cruising speed of 966km/hr, enabling the aircraft to fly non-stop between Europe and the west coast of America. However, the powerplants were plagued with technical issues once the first aircraft entered service. The fan blade tips rubbed on the engine casings initially, which caused constant headaches for the airline's engineering departments.

To oversee the 747 project, Bill Allen came across an up-and-coming engineer and former US Navy veteran named Joe Sutter. He had worked on the Boeing Dash 80 and 707 projects and was considered to be the ideal person to manage the new widebody programme. Dubbed the 'Father of the 747,' as chief engineer, he was to lead the design team for the new aircraft from conception in 1965 to rollout in 1969.

Under Trippe's guidance, in April 1966, Pan American World Airways placed an incredible order with Boeing for 25 of their new airliner, the 747 Jumbo Jet. At $20m dollars each, it was a move that would either make or break the airline and/or the manufacturer. After the announcement, Allen gave a press conference to say that the company had agreed to go ahead with the construction of the jumbo, thanks to the deal with Pan Am.

The world was entering a new era in jet transportation with the quietest and most profitable airliner it had ever known. Many of the world's major airlines, including BOAC, Lufthansa and Japan Air Lines, came knocking on the door in Seattle to see this new phenomenon.

The economics behind the programme were entirely based on the jet's ability to carry large passenger loads over long distances, so the floor area needed to accommodate the large numbers envisioned was not deemed possible with a single-deck fuselage. So the design team, under Sutter, put forward their case for a classic cylindrical

RIGHT: Once the 747 had been towed clear of the hangar, crew members from the participating carriers were given final instructions on when they should crack their bottles of champagne against the fuselage
QANTAS ARCHIVE

BELOW: A brand-new facility to handle the construction of the mammoth airliner was built at Paine Field, 30 miles north of Seattle, at a cost of just over $200m
KEY COLLECTION

a brand-new facility to handle the construction of the mammoth airliner, as existing facilities were too small for the new venture.

After evaluation, one vacant piece of land adjoining Snohomish County Airport in Washington State, more commonly known as Paine Field (a former USAF base), close to the city of Everett and only 30 miles north of Seattle, was deemed perfect for the programme. In June 1966, work began to clear nearly 800 acres of scrubland, with construction of the building beginning during late summer. The completed cost of the new facility came in at just over $200m, and the first technicians took their places during January 1967. A total of 88 firm orders for the aircraft were now in place.

Rollout

As the prototype 747, N7470 (c/n 20235), neared completion, Boeing began to grow increasingly concerned over the aircraft's weight, which had started to creep upwards, threatening to exceed the 2% margin agreed under the contract terms with Pan Am. It was calculated that every 1,000lbs of extra weight would cost $5,000 per aircraft per year in lost payload.

N7470 was rolled out of the factory in Everett under gloomy skies on September 30, 1968. The event was accompanied by speeches and the Everett High School band's performance of Sir Edward Elgar's *Pomp and Circumstance* march. The aircraft wore a striking red and white livery, adorned with a red cheat line, featuring the logos of the 26 airlines that had placed orders. Once the 747 had been towed clear of the hangar, crew members from the participating carriers were given final instructions on when they should crack their bottles of champagne against the fuselage. Everything went according to plan. Even a three-ship formation of Boeing's other products – namely, a 707, 727 and 737 – made a low pass over the airfield to mark the ceremony.

shape, with the flight deck lifted well above the single deck to allow any future cargo versions to have straight-in loading access through an upwards-opening nose cargo door. This new formula had been discussed and agreed with many of the company's customers, who were now more than interested in the new design features.

At a press conference in April 1966, Boeing confirmed that the rollout of the new aircraft was planned for October 1968, with flight tests beginning before the end of that year. Before this could happen, the company needed to construct

BELOW: If it hadn't been for Pan Am's Juan Trippe, there may never have been a Boeing 747. The airline was the jumbo's first customer, ordering 25 in April 1966

With all ground handling tests taken care of, the day finally dawned for the first flight. February 9, 1969, was a momentous day for all concerned, least of all Bill Allen, who knew the biggest »

ABOVE: Due to issues with the early Pratt & Whitney JT9D engines, BOAC managed to recoup some of its losses by leasing out its idle engines to various other operators

gamble in the history of the Boeing Airplane Company was about to unfold. In command of the inaugural flight was Jack Waddell, Boeing's senior experimental test pilot, while assisting him in the right-hand seat was Brien Wygle, assistant director of flight operations, and taking care of the role of flight engineer was Jess Wallick.

The flight lasted 1hr 16mins and everything went as expected – even the troublesome engines behaved as normal. The only slight snag was a loose panel on the starboard flaps, which meant an earlier return to Everett. Nevertheless, everyone was delighted with the day's work.

Ship 1 (N7470) was eventually joined in the test programme by four production models: N747PA (c/n 19639), N731PA (c/n 19637) and N732PA (c/n 19638), all bound for Pan American, and the first example for TWA (Trans World Airways), N93101 (c/n 19667).

The manufacturer chose N731PA *Clipper Bostonia* to make its international debut. The 1969 Paris Air Show promised something special and, at Le Bourget, the crowds waited in anticipation for the arrival of "Le 747 jumbo." Europe had never seen anything as large as the 747, and with orders mounting, the crowds were not disappointed. N731PA arrived in Paris on the morning of June 3, following a 9-hour and 18-minute flight from Seattle and was

parked next to the new Anglo-French supersonic Concorde, which was still in the flight test stage both in France and the United Kingdom.

After displaying the jumbo's unique lines to the rapturous crowd, the crew were given a hero's welcome. The aircraft departed Paris a few days later to return to the Pacific Northwest. The return didn't go exactly as planned because of a problem with one of the Pratt & Whitney JT9Ds, which had to be shut down as the aircraft was close to landing in Seattle. Although she landed with only three engines working, the entire trip to Europe was hailed as a great success. Even more airlines were now thinking the 747 was the way forward, especially to those who held the purse strings in corporate offices. The programme was a success, having taken just over ten months, and there were no major surprises for Sutter and his team. Even with engine reliability issues, the aircraft was proven stable and dependable in all flight regimes. Allen knew he had a winner on his hands.

The first aircraft, N733PA (c/n 19640) *Clipper Young America*, was delivered to Pan Am on schedule and was christened at a ceremony by the US First Lady, Pat Nixon, on January 15, 1970. Six days later, on January 21, the first commercial flight of the widebody was due to take place. *Clipper Young America* was scheduled to operate the flight with the call sign *Clipper 2* with a departure from New York/JFK to London/Heathrow scheduled for 1900hrs.

BELOW: Trans World Airlines or TWA was another early customer for the 747

However, a problem occurred with one of the engines overheating, so a substitute aircraft had to be found. N736PA (c/n 19643) *Clipper Victor* was brought on stand and finally departed in the small hours of January 22, with a complement of 332 passengers and 20 crew on board. The aircraft arrived in London mid-morning to a massive welcome from all concerned. Needless to say, the flight had operated without any problems.

The Boeing 747 was officially now in service.

BOAC innovations

The British Overseas Airways Corporation (BOAC) and its successor, British Airways (BA), enjoyed seamless service with the -136 and -236 and finally the -436 variants of the 747 until the fleet was retired during the COVID-19 pandemic.

In 1968, BOAC had foreseen a need for a larger aircraft to accommodate a rise in passenger numbers. When the Boeing 747 was first on the drawing board, they were one of the initial airlines to pay serious attention to the merits of widebody transportation.

The airline placed an initial order for ten aircraft, with options for a further four. In keeping with many other airlines connected with the project, staff found themselves commuting to and from Seattle as part of the technical team already in-house. Such integration was vital to the planning and design process, as the sheer size of the 747 demanded a rethink over matters such as seating plans, galley arrangements, meal service routines and crew complement, which had risen to 16 compared with eight or nine on the narrowbody fleet.

BOAC had always prided itself on its standard of customer service, so the introduction of the 747 offered opportunities to find new ways to make the onboard experience even better. To oversee the jumbo's entry into service, a dedicated team was formed around Alan Blowers, Ken Thorn and Dave Hughes. A British company called CF Taylor of Wokingham, Berkshire, made new galleys exclusively for the airline. When these were completed, they were shipped directly to Seattle for installation in the aircraft when they were on the production line.

As the first batch of these new modular galleys were mostly handmade, they turned out to be a problematic and expensive choice. Although the concept meant that the whole galley could be unplugged from the refrigeration unit and rolled on and off the aircraft in one piece within a few minutes, problems arose at certain overseas transit stations where catering staff used excessive force in handling the new equipment. Repairing the galleys' down route proved costly, partly because at some stations they didn't have the expertise or knowledge to fix the latest equipment.

The first-class cabin catered for 27 passengers in a style befitting the airline's elite clientele. In addition to the new roll-on/roll-off galleys, three new Herman Smith ovens and a Litton »

ABOVE: Despite receiving its first example in April 1970, a dispute between the airline and its pilots meant that the first three 747s to BOAC sat on the ground for a year before entering service

BELOW: Chief engineer Joe Sutter was dubbed the 'Father of the 747' leading the design team for the new aircraft from conception in 1965 to rollout in 1969 BOEING

Industries microwave oven were installed in the cabin's triangular unit, enabling the highly trained crew to offer a choice of seven entrées from the onboard freezer box. A service trolley offered further main courses, including a carved joint. The first-class crew each carried their own carving set, which was given to them upon completing their first-class training.

The aircraft were also fitted with the first generation of in-flight entertainment, consisting of an 8mm projector housed in the roof of each cabin, screening one movie per sector, a small charge being made for a very basic rubber headset. At each transit stop, In Flight Motion Picture Company representatives would come on board and replace the film reels for the next sector, although on many occasions the system would have a technical fault and a refund would have to be made to passengers.

In Speedbird service

With all systems in place for the launch, BOAC received its first 747-136, G-AWNA (c/n 19761), on April 22, 1970. After an overnight flight from Seattle, the aircraft touched down at London/Heathrow to great fanfare.

RIGHT AND BELOW: The 747 ushered in a new era for BOAC and the airline was keen to find new ways to make the onboard experience even better

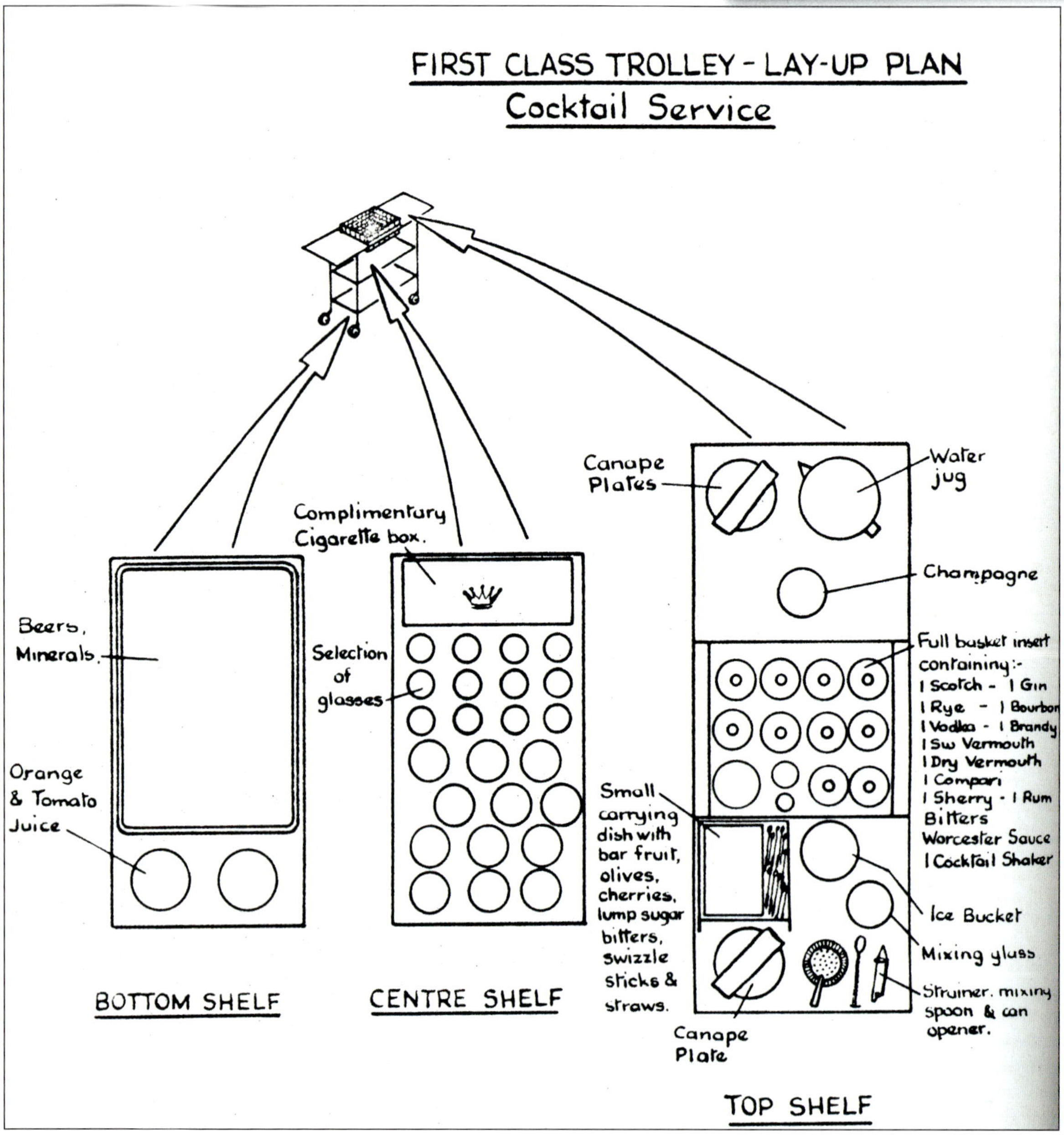

However, due to an industrial dispute between the company and the pilots' union, the British Airline Pilots Association (BALPA), over pay for flying the new aircraft, the 747 was immediately grounded. During the dispute, which lasted over six months, BOAC received some much-needed revenue by leasing its Pratt and Whitney JT9D engines from its first three aircraft (G-AWNA, NB and NC) to other carriers, namely Pan Am, leaving the trio engineless at its Heathrow engineering base with concrete blocks attached to the empty engine pylons.

Even when the pay dispute with the pilots seemed settled, the first scheduled service had to be cancelled an hour before departure because a continuing dispute with a different union meant that no flight engineer reported for duty. The inaugural flight eventually departed on April 14, 1971, when G-AWNF (c/n 19766) took off at 1203hrs local time, bound for New York.

On board, Captain Duggie Redrup took command and was assisted on the flight deck by Captain Leslie Ward, Senior First Officer Penderol Evans and Senior Engineering Officer Lou Boulton. In charge of the cabin, Flight Purser Ron Hollyer directed a specially chosen crew for the momentous occasion.

Initially, the New York service operated twice weekly, then switched to a daily rotation towards the end of the year. As deliveries continued, the 747 took on more routes. By May 1972, a thrice-weekly service to Miami was in operation, as well as a daily flight to Chicago and an eight-hour overnight flight to Nairobi. In early November, Australian services started with the 747, routing via Frankfurt, Beirut, Tehran, Bangkok, Hong Kong and Darwin before terminating at Sydney (twice a week) or Melbourne (once a week). The service soon switched to a daily rotation operating via Bahrain and a technical stop at either Kuala Lumpur or Singapore before flying down to Sydney, where a shuttle service was available for those proceeding to Melbourne.

When BA was formed on March 31, 1974, following the merger of BOAC and British European Airways (BEA), the BOAC branding could still be seen on many of the 747s in the fleet. These colours finally disappeared when G-AWNC (c/n 19763) was given a new coat of paint in February 1977. BA ordered five more of the -136 series before the advent of the longer range -236 equipped with new Rolls-Royce RB211 engines (the first long-range 747, but that's a story for another day).

Both passengers and crew loved the 747. When in service, the author spent 42 happy years flying on all the variants BA operated and as many passengers would often say: "If it's not a Boeing, I'm not going." **AC**

ABOVE: British Airways would go on to operate the -136, -236 and -436 variants of the 747, forming the backbone of the flag carrier's long-haul fleet for decades

BELOW: Wearing a hybrid BOAC/ British Airways livery is G-AWNB (c/n 19762), which was delivered in May 1970 and served with the airline until August 1998

Thanks to Derek Frith and Gerry Manning for their help with this story

Postcards
from Speke

IN THE SWINGING SIXTIES, THE CITY OF LIVERPOOL WAS THE PLACE TO BE WITH ITS VIBRANT MUSIC, ARTS AND FOOTBALL SCENES. FOR AVIATION ENTHUSIASTS, THE CITY'S AIRPORT, NESTLED ON THE BANKS OF THE RIVER MERSEY, WAS ALSO THE PLACE TO SPOT UNUSUAL AIRCRAFT FROM VARIOUS CARRIERS FROM FAR AND WIDE. **BOB O'BRIEN** TAKES US ON A TRIP DOWN MEMORY LANE WITH SOME OF HIS CLASSIC SHOTS.

A classic line-up at Speke in the 1960s shows a de Havilland DH.104 Dove 1B, G-ALVF (c/n 04168), and Douglas C-47 G-AMSS (c/n 32840), both belonging to Dan-Air London, which operated inter-city services across the country
ALL IMAGES VIA BOB O'BRIEN COLLECTION

This British Midland Canadair C-4 Argonaut, G-ALHG (c/n 153), was operating for Arrowsmith Holidays, a Liverpool tour firm. The aircraft was written-off in June 1967, while on approach to Manchester inbound from Palma

An early diversion from Manchester in August 1966 was this Aer Lingus BAC One-Eleven Series 208AL, EI-ANG (c/n BAC.051), seen approaching Runway 26. The jet had been delivered new to the Dublin-based carrier in July 1965 and remained with the airline until 1991

A classic shot from 1966, the year Brazil played Portugal in the FIFA World Cup. Air France Lockheed L-1049G Super Constellation, F-BHBI (c/n 4634), taxies in front of the main terminal at Speke, with a British Eagle Vickers Viscount V.739A, G-ATDR (c/n 393) in the foreground

Another football charter from the mid-1960s, Condor Vickers Viscount V.814, D-ANUN (c/n 338), which had arrived from Frankfurt. The aircraft had originally been delivered to Lufthansa in October 1958, when it operated the airline's first ever Viscount service, before being leased to Condor in 1962

The world's oldest surviving Vickers Viscount, G-ALWF (c/n 5), wore many liveries during its service life, including the colours of Liverpool resident Cambrian Airways

The Ford Motor Company operated many charters over the years. Aviation Traders ATL-98 Carvair, G-AOFW (c/n 10351), was inbound from the continent wearing the colours of British United Airways (BUA) during a rare visit to Speke

Dan-Air flew between Liverpool and Amsterdam for a brief period during the 1960s. Seen following its arrival from the Dutch capital is de Havilland DH.106 Comet 4, G-APDJ (c/n 6429), with a very light passenger load

Diverted due to fog at Manchester/Ringway was this BOAC Vickers VC10 Standard, G-ARVB (c/n 805), which arrived from Prestwick before continuing its journey to Heathrow

Seen receiving maintenance is this British Eagle de Havilland DH.104 Dove, G-AROI (c/n 04474) *Eaglet*. After entering service on July 4, 1966, the aircraft operated a twice-daily scheduled service between Dundee and Glasgow to connect with scheduled services to London/Heathrow

Vickers Vanguard 953, G-APEN (c/n 717), wearing BEA's iconic Red Square livery, seen taxiing for departure after a weather-related diversion from Manchester. Note the Autair BAC One-Eleven in the background that would eventually fly for Cambrian Airways

Bringing the Budapest Honvéd FC team to Liverpool was this Malev Hungarian Airlines Ilyushin Il-14P, HA-MAD (c/n 14803028)

After completing its lease with Air France, this Vickers Viscount V.739, G-ATDU (c/n 87), belonging to British Eagle, is seen outside the airline's maintenance base in September 1968. The aircraft was repainted in British Eagle colours and named *City of Liverpool*, but was withdrawn from use in November 1968 following the airline's collapse

A very rare image of a Treffield International Airlines Viscount V.812, G-ATVR (c/n 365). The aircraft had been leased to the short-lived East Midlands-based airline from Channel Airways in April 1967

This Airspeed AS.57 Ambassador 2, G-AMAG (c/n 5229), of Dan-Air London awaits its next load of passengers. The aircraft was written-off on September 30, 1968, during a landing incident at London/Gatwick, which caused a diversion to Manston Airport, where it made a wheels-up landing

Bristol 175 Britannia 309, G-ANCH (c/n 12924), spent many months at Speke in the colours of Ghana Airways in 1968 after being leased to British Eagle. It was later taken up by Monarch Airlines before being withdrawn from use in April 1972

This KLM Royal Dutch Airlines Convair CV-340-48, PH-CGF (c/n 114), arriving from Amsterdam/Schiphol on a football charter

Captured on Speke's western apron is this Bristol 170-Freighter 31E, EI-APC (c/n 13072), belonging to Irish airline Aer Turas. The aircraft also flew with the Irish flag carrier Aer Lingus and BKS Air Transport

Another carrier that used Speke for diversions was SAS Scandinavian Airline System. This Sud Aviation SE210 Caravelle III, OY-KRG (c/n 191), arrived from Copenhagen before continuing to Dublin with a reduced load

Looking resplendent in the colours of Manx Airlines is this BAC One-Eleven Series 304AX, G-WLAD (c/n BAC.112), which had just arrived on a scheduled service from the Isle of Man. The jet had previously been based at Speke with British Eagle, before joining Manx's owner British Midland in 1985

Wearing the latter colours of Cambrian Airways is this Vickers Viscount V.701, G-AMOJ (c/n 23). In the background, another Viscount wears the British Air Services scheme, of which Cambrian had become part in November 1967

BEA Hawker Siddeley HS-121 Trident 3B, G-AWZA (c/n 2302), was one of several aircraft that took part in blind landing trials at Speke before the equipment was taken out and installed at Manchester

Charter Champions –
LTU's TriStars

GERMAN CHARTER OPERATOR LTU EXPANDED RAPIDLY IN THE 1970S, OPERATING A SIZEABLE FLEET OF NEW AND USED LOCKHEED L-1011S. LEE CROSS TELLS THE STORY OF THE TRISTARS THAT WORE THE AIRLINE'S FAMOUS RED AND WHITE LIVERY

Lufttransport Union was founded on October 20, 1955, to cater to the growing German charter market. Initially, it offered flights from Hamburg, Düsseldorf, Frankfurt, Stuttgart, and Munich to destinations across Europe and the Canary Islands. In April 1956, the name was changed to Lufttransport-Unternehmen (companies) or LTU for short.

The airline expanded steadily as the country experienced a surge in foreign travel demand following its reconstruction after World War Two. LTU added its first jet aircraft, the Sud Aviation Caravelle III, on February 5, 1965 and became one of the launch customers for the Fokker F-28 Fellowship, with the first example joining the fleet on February 17, 1969.

By the end of the 1960s, LTU was one of the first charter airlines in the world to operate an all-jet fleet, and as the carrier entered the 1970s, management looked to expand the network to compete with the mighty German carrier Lufthansa.

Enter the TriStars

In 1971, LTU carried 500,000 passengers, and the airline watched with interest as, in October of that year, UK charter operator Court Line signed a letter of intent for two all-economy Lockheed L-1011 TriStars for use on its high-density charter routes, as well as opening up new transatlantic destinations.

This was the age of the 'jumbo jet', with a new wave of wide-bodied airliners being unveiled by aircraft manufacturers, and LTU looked at them

BELOW: LTU received its first L-1011 TriStar, D-AERA (c/n 193R-1033), in May 1973. It was retired by LTU in April 1981 and served with Eastern Air Lines, American Trans Air and Cathay Pacific, amongst others LOCKHEED MARTIN

> **"By the end of the 1960s, LTU was one of the first charter airlines in the world to operate an all-jet fleet"**

ABOVE: The first undelivered PSA L-1011 to join the LTU fleet, D-AERI (c/n 193L-1114), arrived at Düsseldorf in March 1977, becoming the third TriStar in the fleet AIRTEAMIMAGES.COM/ CARL FORD

all. However, it quickly focused on Lockheed's offering, as the Boeing 747 was deemed too large, while the McDonnell Douglas DC-10 was viewed as technically inferior and unable to meet the airline's requirements. So, in October 1972, LTU ordered two TriStar 1s, with the first example, D-AERA (c/n 193R-1033), arriving at the carrier's Düsseldorf base on May 29, 1973. After completing some crew training, the 362-seat jet

entered revenue service on June 14, operating flights from Düsseldorf to Ibiza.

But the new airliner wasn't without its problems. In those days, the arrival of an aircraft with more than 300 passengers at a small Mediterranean airport not yet equipped to handle such a large volume of people often meant congestion of passenger and ground handling facilities. To combat this problem, LTU took up »

ABOVE: The lower-deck lounge on the ex-PSA TriStars remained in use until 1983. Known as the 'Club Lounge', the exclusive area featured a leather-framed bar, sofa-style seats, and could accommodate 16 passengers, who had the option to upgrade for a small fee. Meals were served on china, accompanied by extra snacks and complimentary alcoholic drinks LOCKHEED MARTIN

the option of integral rear airstairs in the main aft cargo hold, which could be extended without outside assistance. The TriStars also came with an electric baggage-loading belt for luggage and cargo. However, these features meant additional weight and thus increased fuel and maintenance costs. As the airports gradually developed, these features were removed.

LTU received its second L-1011, D-AERO (c/n 193A-1008), in November 1975. The 358-seat jet was an ex-Eastern Air Lines example (N307EA). It had been parked up by the carrier due to the ongoing global recession brought on by the 1973 oil crisis, which had created overcapacity for many airlines, particularly in the US.

PSA's unwanted aircraft

Another airline that was struggling was Pacific Southwest Airlines (PSA), which had ordered five L-1011s for its high-density California routes in 1970. After receiving two examples, which were subsequently grounded due to their high operating costs when fuel prices had tripled, the airline then refused to take delivery of the final three it had on order. This meant that Lockheed was left with three TriStars, built with an interior designed specifically for PSA, including a

lower-level passenger lounge converted from the cargo hold and lower deck galley areas, which made the models incredibly difficult to sell.

Despite filing a lawsuit against PSA, the manufacturer worked with the airline to market the redundant aircraft, creating a full-colour brochure in June 1975 which promoted their specific design for short-haul commuter operations or charters. Included were provisions for the installation of galley areas on the main

"It quickly focused on Lockheed's offering, as the Boeing 747 was deemed too large, while the McDonnell Douglas DC-10 was viewed as technically inferior and unable to meet the airline's requirements"

D-AERN (c/n 193A-1158), which had originally been delivered to Eastern Air Lines in November 1978, was also converted to a -200 series, offering extra range, which allowed the airline to launch direct flights from Munich to New York AIRTEAMIMAGES.COM/WORLD AVIATION ARCHIVE

ABOVE: Built as a TriStar 1, D-AERU (c/n 193L-1125) was converted to a -100 series before being delivered in October 1977 AIRTEAMIMAGES.COM/ CAZ CASWELL

deck, although no offers were made to remove the downstairs lounge configuration. A sale to Avianca Airlines of Colombia fell through in August 1976.

Discussions then began with LTU, and in October that year, an agreement was made to return its two initial TriStar 1s and replace them with the three undelivered jets. This would provide the German carrier with a high-density layout, perfect for its charter operations, with a consistent standard of cabin configuration across the fleet.

D-AERO was returned to Lockheed on April 18, 1977, but would subsequently be returned to the German carrier's fleet in February 1979, before joining Eastern Air Lines in 1981. The jet then returned to LTU in November 1985, albeit under the new registration of D-AERY, and remained in the fleet until February 20, 1995. D-AERA meanwhile stayed with LTU until November 1979, when it went on to fly for Nigeria Airways.

The first ex-PSA L-1011 to be delivered was N10115 (c/n 193L-1114), which arrived at Düsseldorf on March 18, 1977. With its D-Check (heavy maintenance) completed, a full repaint in LTU colours and re-registering as D-AERI, the jet entered passenger service a few days later.

Carpet catastrophe

But disaster struck when, on the evening of June 28, 1991, while undergoing carpet replacement at the airline's engineering facility at Düsseldorf Airport, a fire broke out in D-AERI's cabin. As the fire took hold, the maintenance team managed to push the TriStar out of the hangar, still attached to the tug, while they waited for firefighters to arrive. The intense heat caused the cabin roof to melt and collapse, resulting in a total hull loss. All usable parts were removed, and the remains were later dismantled. Part of the wing was donated to the aircraft museum in Hermeskeil, and the cockpit was given to the Technical University in Braunschweig.

As a replacement, the airline took in another Eastern example, N329EA (c/n 193A-1085), on July 8, 1991, re-registering the jet as D-AERC and painting it in a hybrid livery, with LTU red adorning the former operator's iconic

'hockey-stick' scheme. The jet entered revenue service on July 21, operating from Düsseldorf to Palma, and remained with the carrier until November 6, 1992.

Throughout the years of operating the Lockheed TriStars, LTU also provided outstanding expertise in maintenance and training of the type. The airline had a large hangar at Düsseldorf, in which up to three L-1011s could be housed simultaneously. A, B and C checks were all carried out here, with US carrier Hawaiian Airlines, among others, using the facility for its TriStar fleet.

The second ex-PSA jet to arrive was N10116 (c/n 193L-1120), handed over on May 12, 1977. The trijet was re-registered D-AERE and would remain with LTU until May 8, 1995. D-AERU (c/n 193L-1125) was the third and final ex-PSA L-1011 (ex-N10117) and landed at Düsseldorf on October 25, 1977, serving the airline until November 29, 1994.

In 1978, thanks to the introduction of the TriStars, the airline reached the milestone of carrying one million passengers per year. By October 1979, the last Caravelle was sold off, leaving the L-1011 as LTU's sole aircraft type.

Despite reservations about the lower-deck lounge, it remained in use until 1983, when it was removed by Eastern Air Lines engineers in Miami. Known as the 'Club Lounge', the exclusive area was accessed by a staircase from the forward cabin. It featured a leather-framed bar, sofa-style seats, and, since there were no windows, two illuminated picture frames displaying an exotic, sun-kissed Spanish landscape. The lounge could accommodate 16 passengers, who had the option to upgrade for a small fee, with meals served on china plates, extra snacks, and complimentary alcoholic drinks.

Eastern agreement

As Eastern Air Lines continued to struggle financially due to competition from new airlines following the US deregulation act and labour unrest, the American carrier reached an agreement with LTU to offer additional TriStars to the German carrier during its peak summer season.   »

BELOW: LTU went on to order six Airbus A330-300s, with the first being introduced into service on January 23, 1995. The new state-of-the-art Airbus jets signalled the end of the TriStars after 23 years of loyal service KEY-TONY DIXON

By 1988, LTU had overtaken Condor as West Germany's number one charter airline. Condor had introduced the TriStar's rival, the McDonnell Douglas DC-10, in late 1979 **CONDOR**

D-AERN (c/n 193A-1158) was originally delivered to the Miami-based carrier in November 1978 as N339EA before joining LTU in December 1980. It was immediately leased back to its original operator before returning to Germany on March 20, 1981. This particular aircraft was later converted to a -200 series in April 1986, allowing LTU to offer direct flights from Munich to New York. This was the only one of this variant flown by the carrier and would remain in the fleet until November 9, 1995.

D-AERM (c/n 193A-1153), ex-N338EA, was delivered to LTU on January 4, 1981 and served until July 1995. D-AERP (c/n 193A-1152) was another ex-Eastern (ex-N337EA) example, which arrived at Düsseldorf on April 22, 1982 and stayed until November 12, 1993.

Eastern Air Lines also leased TriStar 1, N323EA (c/n 193A-1045) to LTU on June 3, 1988. The jet operated in a hybrid livery of the two carriers, similar to D-AERC, and remained with the airline until November 27, when it was transferred to Cathay Pacific.

Opening up the world

As the TriStars arrived, LTU was able to expand into long-haul operations, launching flights to Miami in November 1976. Services were also added to New York and Los Angeles in May 1977, with both Sri Lanka and Bangkok joining

BELOW: TriStar 500, D-AERV (c/n 193Y-1195), was an ex-Pan Am example. When it was delivered to LTU in April 1989, it wore this unique colour scheme, with a white overall fuselage and red cheatline along the window line, inherited from its previous operator AIRTEAMIMAGES.COM/ MARTIN BOSCHHUIZEN

ABOVE: The McDonnell Douglas MD-11 was seen as the successor for LTU's TriStar fleet, and four of the type joined the carrier between December 1991 and March 1993 AIRTEAMIMAGES.COM/ WOLFGANG MENDORF

the network as its first Asian destinations in November of that year.

As the travel companies that used LTU for their charter flights considered broadening the range of destinations they offered, the airline considered purchasing an aircraft that could provide non-stop flights.

The TriStar 1s had served the airline well. Still, refuelling stops and crew changes had to be made on many flights with the airline utilising Shannon (Ireland), Gander (Canada), Manama (Bahrain) or Santa Maria (Azores) airports.

In May 1979, LTU ordered two all-economy, 288-seat TriStar 500s for delivery the following year. The first -500 to arrive was D-AERT (c/n 193J-1183) on April 14, 1980 and was joined by sister-ship D-AERL (c/n 193J-1196) on October 27.

A third -500 series was added on April 14, 1989. D-AERV (c/n 193Y-1195) had originally served with Pan Am and subsequently United Airlines, when the latter took over Pan Am's Pacific division in 1985. It was painted in a livery based on the previous owner's colour scheme and remained with the airline until February 12, 1994. Apart from these three -500s and the converted -200, the rest of LTU's TriStars were -1s.

By 1988 LTU had overtaken Condor as West Germany's number one charter airline carrying over 3.5m passengers per year. At this time, approximately 18% of the airline's capacity was allocated to long-haul operations.

TriStar Memories

Over the years, the TriStars proved a massive hit with both passengers and crews, as LTU purser and cabin crew trainer Rainer Jünger recalls: "Everyone who flew on our L-1011s loved them. They were comfortable, quiet and had an exquisite safety record. Cockpit crews loved the technical standard of the jet, which was way ahead of its time, and for us, cabin crew, we loved the spaciousness of the cabin, even after a few increased seat configurations."

One feature of the L-1011 which proved particularly popular with cabin crew was the downstairs galley on the early TriStar 1s, as Jünger explained: "This position, known as the G1, turned out to be the favourite among the TriStar crews. This crew member was not involved with the service in the main cabin; instead, they sent up all the necessary service equipment using the TriStar's twin elevators. This, sadly, all changed with the introduction of the -500 series, where the galley was moved upstairs. But the spacious cabin remained unchanged and made our cabin work quite comfortable." »

BELOW: In June 1988, Eastern leased TriStar 1, N323EA (c/n 193A-1045) to LTU for the summer season. It is seen here at Düsseldorf wearing a hybrid Eastern/LTU livery AIRTEAMIMAGES.COM/ WOLFGANG MENDORF

"The airline had a large hangar at Düsseldorf, in which up to three L-1011s could be housed simultaneously. A, B and C checks were all carried out here, with US carrier Hawaiian Airlines, among others, using the facility for its TriStar fleet"

Reg'n	Type	C/n	Delivery date	Notes
D-AERA	Lockheed L-1011 TriStar 1	193R-1033	29/5/1973	-
D-AERO	Lockheed L-1011 TriStar 1	193A-1008	8/11/1975	Ex-Eastern Airlines (N307EA) Later re-registered as D-AERY
D-AERI	Lockheed L-1011 TriStar 1	193L-1114	18/3/1977	Destroyed by fire during reoutine maintainence at DUS 28/06/1991
D-AERE	Lockheed L-1011 TriStar 1	193L-1120	12/5/1977	-
D-AERU	Lockheed L-1011 TriStar 100	193L-1125	25/10/1977	Converted from a TriStar 1 to a TriStar 100 prior to delivery
D-AERN	Lockheed L-1011 TriStar 200	193A-1158	1/12/1980	Converted from a TriStar 1 to a TriStar 200 in April 1986
D-AERM	Lockheed L-1011 TriStar 1	193A-1153	4/1/1981	-
D-AERP	Lockheed L-1011 TriStar 1	193A-1152	22/4/1982	-
D-AERT	Lockheed L-1011 TriStar 500	193J-1183	14/4/1980	-
D-AERL	Lockheed L-1011 TriStar 500	193J-1196	27/10/1980	-
D-AERV	Lockheed L-1011 TriStar 500	193Y-1195	14/4/1989	-
D-AERC	Lockheed L-1011 TriStar 1	193A-1085	8/7/1991	Ex-Eastern Airlines N329EA to replace D-AERI. Wore a hybrid Eastern/LTU livery
N323EA	Lockheed L-1011 TriStar 1	193A-1045	3/6/1988	Leased from Eastern Airlines for 1988 summer season. Wore a hybrid Eastern/LTU livery

Indeed, they proved so popular that LTU went on to promote its new MD-11 as the 'TriJet' in an attempt to maintain a public perception of commonality with its predecessor.

However, LTU quickly discovered that the MD-11 alone would be insufficient to replace its L-1011s, which had been able to efficiently perform a wide range of tasks over the years, from short hops to the Mediterranean to long trips across the Atlantic and Indian Oceans.

In addition to the MD-11, LTU went on to order six Airbus A330-300s, the first of which, D-AERF (c/n 082) was introduced on the Düsseldorf to Larnaca route on January 23, 1995. The new state-of-the-art Airbus jets signalled the end of the TriStars after 23 years of loyal service, and the last example, D-AERL, was retired from the fleet on April 30, 1996.

Much of the success of LTU was down to the Lockheed L-1011 TriStars or the 'Lady of the Skies', as many LTU crew referred to her. It transformed the carrier, opening the iconic red-liveried airline up to the world, creating one of the largest charter airlines in the industry at the time and one of the most popular brands in Germany.

In March 2007, Air Berlin took over, and the LTU name disappeared from the skies forever. Speaking of his time working on the TriStars, Jünger told the author fondly: "After 32 great years, LTU merged into Air Berlin, where I remained for another eight years until its insolvency started my retirement. I now look back at 40 wonderful years of aviation, but among all the different aircraft types I have operated, the L-1011 TriStar always remains my number one." **A**

The airline also developed a good relationship with the Maldives and to protect the island's delicate ecosystem from the thousands of tourists LTU brought in, the airline used to transport large quantities of waste in the holds of the TriStars for disposal back in Germany. As a gesture of goodwill, the Maldives Post Office issued stamps and postcards showing an LTU TriStar in flight over the islands.

By spring 1993, the worldwide TriStar fleet had passed the 10 million flight hours milestone, and it was an LTU -500 series example, D-AERT, which broke the individual high-time record, logging 61,000 flying hours.

Time for a replacement

As LTU entered the 1990s, it joined IATA and began operating scheduled flights to the United States, Bangkok, and Sri Lanka, aiming to further compete with Lufthansa.

Technologically newer and more fuel-efficient aircraft were coming online, and to keep up with its rivals, LTU looked at replacing its now ageing TriStar fleet. The McDonnell Douglas MD-11 was chosen as the only real successor, and four of the type: D-AERB (c/n 48484), D-AERW (c/n 48485), D-AERX (c/n 48486) and D-AERZ (c/n 48538) joined the carrier between December 1991 and March 1993.

The Lockheed TriStars had been seen as the symbol of the German carrier through the years.

BELOW: Much of the success of LTU was down to the Lockheed L-1011 TriStars or the 'Lady of the Skies', as many LTU crew referred to her, which opened up the iconic red-liveried airline to the world **LOCKHEED MARTIN**

Convair's 880 Jet-Liner is the champion of the jets. It is the world's newest, fastest and most versatile passenger plane.
CONVAIR
A DIVISION OF GENERAL DYNAMICS CORPORATION
First to offer Convair 880 or 600-Coronado Jet-Liner service will be TWA, DELTA, REAL-AEROVIAS (Brazil), S.A.S., SWISSAIR, AMERICAN, C.A.T. (Formosa), CAPITAL, AVENSA (Venezuela)

BA *in the* regions

ONCE A COMMON SIGHT AT AIRPORTS ACROSS THE UK, THE HISTORY OF BRITISH AIRWAYS' REGIONAL OPERATION IS A COMPLEX ONE, AS LEE CROSS EXPLAINS

When the British Overseas Airways Corporation (BOAC), British European Airways (BEA), Cambrian Airways and Northeast Airlines merged in March 1974 to form British Airways (BA), the new national carrier inherited a vast but somewhat underperforming domestic route network.

For two years following the merger, BA kept Cambrian and Northeast, along with BEA's Scottish Airways and Channel Islands divisions, as separate entities. Aircraft were painted in BA's first livery, designed by Negus & Negus, while the names of the regional partners were added above the passenger door. However, on April 1, 1976, the four divisions were merged into a single regional operation in a bid to streamline its services and stem losses.

Fleet upgrade

One of the first issues for BA to tackle was its fleet, particularly the ageing Vickers Viscounts, many of which had been in service for around two decades. BA had inherited 37 Viscounts following the merger, consisting of 35 V.800s and a pair of V.701s. A suitable replacement for the venerable Viscount was hard to find. Still, the Hawker Siddeley HS 748 quickly proved its worth after BA ordered two 46-seat Series-2As in 1974, the carrier's first aircraft order following the merger. The duo entered service in August 1975 and were used to replace the Viscounts on the lucrative North Sea oil routes, linking Aberdeen with Kirkwall, Glasgow and Lerwick. The last of these services benefitted greatly from the type's ability to uplift a full payload compared to the restricted Viscounts.

BELOW: The British Aircraft Corporation One-Eleven formed the backbone of the BA regional fleet for many years. G-AZMF (c/n BAC.240) was one of 13 Series 500s inherited following the acquisition of British Caledonian in December 1987 AIRTEAMIMAGES.COM/ KEITH BLINCOW

ABOVE: British Airways inherited 37 Viscounts, consisting of 35 V.800s and a pair of V.701s
BA HERITAGE CENTRE

As more Viscounts left the fleet, additional HS 748s, affectionately known as 'Budgies', were obtained. Despite their small size and ageing design, frequent travellers and the crews who flew them were impressed by the HS 748, noting how it could fly in weather "when even the seagulls were grounded." During the summer months, the Rolls-Royce Dart-powered prop could be found on some lengthier services from Scotland to the Channel Islands, as well as on cross-border services to Birmingham, Bristol and Manchester. At the last two bases and Glasgow,

BA had divided up the 18 British Aircraft Corporation (BAC) One-Eleven Series 500s and four Series 400s to operate the increasing number of scheduled and weekend charter services.

At Birmingham, new routes included Brussels, Frankfurt and Copenhagen, which were former British Midland services, taken over as part of a route swap in 1978. In return, BA had handed over its services from Liverpool to the Isle of Man, Belfast, London/Heathrow and the Channel Islands. Aberdeen and Milan were also added to the network.

New decade

The early 1980s were a difficult period for BA. A planned privatisation had been delayed as the ongoing oil crisis had plunged the airline deep into debt. Savage cost-cutting ensued, affecting all areas of the operation. Domestic regional services from several airports were cut entirely, including Bristol, Cardiff, Guernsey, the Isle of Man, Leeds/Bradford, Liverpool and Southampton. Several independent carriers such as Dan-Air, British Caledonian and Brymon Airways stepped in to take over the former routes, although many of these would subsequently be swallowed up by the flag carrier years later.

In 1982, BA established its Highland Division, an autonomous unit to oversee the airline's Scottish services. The final Viscount left the fleet in May 1982 after three additional HS 748s were acquired to replace them. The Budgies served with BA until 1992, when the final example, G-HDBD (c/n 1797), was retired. During its 17 years of service, the type transformed the Scottish division, making it a profitable part of the regional network.

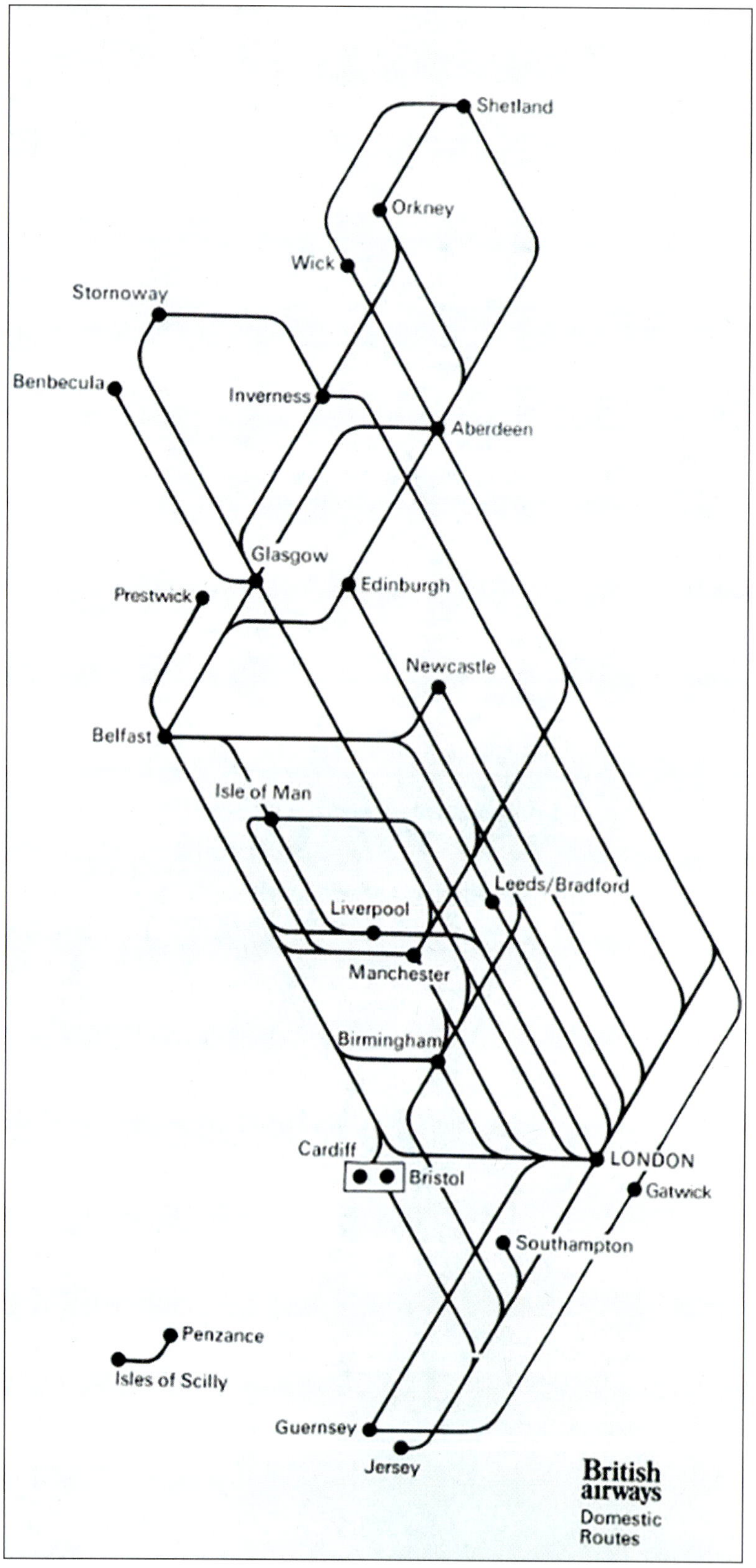

The same could not be said of BA's Channel Islands operation. Following the merger, 14 destinations were served from Jersey, including Amsterdam and London/Heathrow, flown by ex-Northeast Airlines Tridents. But as the Viscounts left the fleet, the routes were dropped, leaving just Manchester and Heathrow served by One-Elevens. Guernsey was removed from the schedule entirely.

At Birmingham, routes to Copenhagen, Milan and Zurich were cut. However, in 1983, a new start-up known as Birmingham Executive Airways stepped in to fill the gap.

ABOVE: A route map of BA's domestic network from 1978 shows the vast number of UK and Channel Islands airports the flag carrier served at the time
BA HERITAGE CENTRE

As privatisation loomed for the flag carrier, grants were awarded to regional airlines to start competitive services, only adding to BA's regional financial woes. Birmingham Executive subsequently launched Amsterdam, Stuttgart, Düsseldorf and Frankfurt in 1986. Rather than compete, BA chose to co-operate with the carrier on several routes.

'Boomingham'

Keen to continue streamlining the regional operation and buoyed by the success of its Shuttle service (see *BA Shuttle*), management looked at introducing the hub-and-spoke concept, already popular in the US, to the UK market. Instead of offering direct flights from regional airports, BA planned to seamlessly route domestic passengers through its Birmingham and Manchester hubs onto a network of flights across Europe. An initial trial proved successful and, in February 1988, it was announced that a new dedicated terminal would be built at Birmingham International Airport.

The new facility opened its doors in July 1991, becoming the world's first terminal to integrate both domestic and international arrivals, with minimum transfer times of just 30 minutes. BA based 13 aircraft here and its extensive network across the UK and Europe was supported by franchise partners, Birmingham European Airways (rebranded from Birmingham Executive in August 1989) and Brymon Airways. The former, now owned by The Plimsoll Line (TPL), a holding company which also co-owned Brymon with BA, had taken on four of the flag carriers' ex-One Eleven Series 400s and several former routes, including Amsterdam and Belfast, under a codeshare agreement.

Christmas Eve 1992, and then from Birmingham, with G-BJRU (c/n BAC.238) departing in June 1993. The older Series 400s had already been retired by October 1988, replaced with 13 Series 500s inherited following the acquisition of British Caledonian Airways in December 1987.

The One-Elevens were replaced by 106-seat Boeing 737-236s, transferred from Heathrow, as the mainline division began receiving its brand new 737-436s in October 1991. To promote the launch of BA Regional, several of the -236s had *Birmingham* or *Manchester* titles added to the fuselage to denote their bases.

Birmingham European struggled financially and was subsequently merged with Plymouth-based Brymon to form Brymon European Airways, aiming to create a more resilient carrier. The combined entity launched operations in »

A year after Eurohub opened its doors, BA advertised the Midlands hub as 'Boomingham' and, along with its partners, carried some 40% of the airport's scheduled traffic at its peak.

But BA's regional finances were far from booming. A further restructuring took place in March 1992, with the creation of yet another new subsidiary to take on the operations, BA Regional. This entailed the complete withdrawal of the One-Eleven fleet, first from Manchester, with the last, G-AVMW (c/n BAC.150), leaving on

ABOVE: Some 737s had *Birmingham* titles added, including G-BKYG (c/n 23165) *River Exe*

BELOW: BAe ATP G-BTPL (c/n 2402) *Strathspey* was delivered to the airline in January 1992, one of 13 operated by the flag carrier

BA CityFlyer

London/Gatwick-based CityFlyer Express became BA's first franchise partner in August 1993 in a first-of-a-kind deal for the UK airline industry. The initial five-year agreement proved a success, with CityFlyer carrying some 7 million passengers each year for the flag carrier. In 1999, it was taken over by BA in a deal valued at around £75m and subsequently absorbed into BA's mainline short-haul operation from Gatwick. Three years later, CityFlyer Express was integrated into BA's new regional offshoot BA CitiExpress, later remodelled as a low-cost carrier and rebranded as BA Connect. When the latter was sold to Flybe in late 2006, the flag carrier announced that it would resurrect the CityFlyer brand under a new AOC to focus on the London/City operations. BA had begun serving the Docklands facility in November 1999 through its franchise partner BRAL with a thrice-daily service to Sheffield. It introduced its own services to London/City in April 2003, with flights to Glasgow, followed soon after by Paris and Frankfurt.

ABOVE: The Hawker Siddeley HS 748 was deemed a suitable replacement for the Viscount and the newly formed BA ordered its first two 46-seat Series-2As in 1974, the new carrier's first aircraft order KEY COLLECTION

October 1992, but less than a year later it was disbanded. BA took over the original Brymon assets, making it a wholly-owned subsidiary and rebranding it as British Airways Express. Meanwhile, the AP Moller Maersk Group bought the Birmingham European share and rebranded it as Maersk Air UK, which continued as a full franchise partner. Indeed, the One-Eleven, which had proved ideal for BA's regional operations continued to operate in its iconic Landor scheme with Maersk Air UK until August 1998.

Up north

North of the border, BA's Highland Division was now utilising the new BAe Advanced Turboprop (ATP) as a replacement for its HS 748s. The airline had ordered eight examples, with options on eight more in 1988, to be used specifically for its Scottish

routes and Inter German services. Deliveries began in December that year and, by July 1989, four of the 64-seat turboprops had been delivered to its Glasgow base, with four others going to Germany. Despite teething problems, another five were ordered from the manufacturer in 1991. When the four returned from Germany following the reunification and the end of internal services, BA would go on to boast a fleet of 13 ATPs.

In 1992, British Airways Regional launched long-haul services from Birmingham, Glasgow and Manchester. The latter had boasted a varied long-haul network over the years, including Boeing 747 flights to New York, Montreal and Toronto, and Lockheed L-1011 TriStar services to Barbados, Orlando, Hong Kong, Mumbai and Islamabad. However, these services had been operated by BA's main line.

Three dedicated Boeing 767-336ERs were transferred to BA Regional – G-BNWN (c/n 25444), G-BNWO (c/n 25442) and G-BNWU (c/n 25829) – to operate the routes. Manchester and Birmingham boasted daily flights to New York/ JFK, although the latter service was routed via Glasgow three times per week.

Later, Manchester gained a five-times-weekly services to Los Angeles. However, this was dropped by the end of the summer 1994 season due to low yields. By January 1995, the long-haul fleet had shrunk to a single 767, based at Manchester and a pair of Boeing 757-236s stationed at Birmingham and Glasgow. The 757s had been refitted with a spacious 158-seat cabin, featuring 18 Club World seats in the forward cabin and a spacious economy section. They were used on daily services from Birmingham to New York and onwards to Toronto, and from Glasgow to New York and onwards to Boston. However, by the end of October 1998, these services too were withdrawn.

By the early 1990s, Manchester boasted a network of 32 destinations, offering 270 flights per week. The airline was keen to recreate its Eurohub concept in the northwest and announced a £75m investment to create its own terminal, housing all its services under one roof and offering 30-minute connections.

Designed by Grimshaw Architects, the terminal, which had previously been the domestic pier opened by Princess Diana in 1989, boasted 20 airbridge stands and a mezzanine lounge surrounded by floor-to-ceiling windows. It opened in May 1998 and a year later was

ABOVE: Brymon European Airways BAC One-Eleven Series 400, G-AWBL (c/n BAC.132), taxies out from Birmingham's Eurohub terminal. The airline had been created following the merger of Birmingham European and Brymon Airways ALL IMAGES KEITH GASKELL UNLESS STATED

RIGHT: Wearing BA's 'Grand Union' World Tails livery is the appropriately registered G-XBHX (c/n 28572), which was one of several Boeing 737-300s leased by the airline while it evaluated the long-term fleet replacement for its 737-236 fleet

operating as a hub-and-spoke facility, with waves of flights throughout the day arriving from domestic destinations, offering passengers the opportunity to connect onto European flights. Manchester had grown to offer the third biggest network of schedules for British Airways after Heathrow and Gatwick. At one stage, it offered an incredible 33 flights each day to the capital.

Before the terminal's opening, British Airways had begun looking at a replacement for its ageing

ABOVE: Wearing a modified BA Landor livery before the introduction of its controversial World Tails, this BAe Jetstream 41 G-MSKJ (c/n 41034) was operated by Birmingham-based franchise partner Maersk Air UK

737-236 fleet. As an interim measure, it leased seven Boeing 737-300s while it evaluated its long-term fleet strategy.

A year later, BA announced its intention to order 59 Airbus A320 Family jets, including several A319s which were earmarked for its regional operations. Birmingham became the first base to receive the A319 in 1999.

Widening the franchise

Despite still retaining its own fleet of aircraft, BA's regional operations had been gradually handed over to more franchise partners. Alongside Brymon and Maersk Air UK, BA had signed up Scottish regional carrier Loganair as a partner in July 1994. Its fleet of Britten-Norman Islanders, Shorts 360s and de Havilland Canada DHC-6 Twin Otters were painted in full British Airways colours, with BA flight numbers added to the Scottish services.

Loganair was part of the Airlines of Britain Group, owned by BA rival British Midland, which also included Manx Airlines (Europe), a Cardiff-based subsidiary of the Isle of Man carrier. In 1994, it was announced that BA was looking to take in a franchise partner to operate some of its domestic services, primarily from its Manchester base. In January 1995, Manx Airlines (Europe) was named as the chosen carrier, with its fleet of BAe ATPs and Jetstream 41s wearing British Airways Express colours. During its first year of operations, the new addition to the franchise carried 1.2 million passengers and reintroduced the flag carrier to many UK and Irish airports that had not seen a BA aircraft for many years.

Just over a year later, the Airlines of Britain Group was disbanded and British Regional Airlines (BRAL) was created to operate the BA Express services of Manx Airlines (Europe) and Loganair. However, the latter was sold in a management buyout in March 1997, but continued as a BA franchise partner until October 2008. At the same time, BA closed down its Highlands and Islands division and transferred all its operations to BRAL.

BA Shuttle

On January 12, 1975, the first British Airways Shuttle service took off from Heathrow bound for Glasgow. The shuttle concept had already proven a success in the US, with passengers able to turn up at the gate ten minutes before departure and guarantee themselves a seat on a flight. Management of the newly formed British Airways was keen to emulate this success and bring the concept to the UK.

Initially, nine of the carrier's Hawker Siddeley Trident 1s were allocated for the operation, which involved hourly flights between the two cities on weekdays. The Trident's auto-land capabilities proved invaluable for the operation, and BA highlighted the UK's changeable weather conditions when promoting the service. The service proved a success – a year after launching, some 1.2 million passengers were being carried.

Edinburgh was added to the schedule in April 1976, followed by Belfast a year later and Manchester in 1979. By this point, One-Elevens and 737s could be found on the route, and during busier times, 747s or L-1011 TriStars were brought in. Occasionally, it would even deploy its flagship Concorde on the routes to position the supersonic airliner for its lucrative charter flights.

BA even planned to extend the shuttle concept beyond the UK to its key European services, with flights to Paris and Brussels mooted. Discussions began with regulatory bodies and rival airlines such as Air France and Sabena. Sadly, talks fell apart and BA never extended the service.

In August 1983, BA launched the upgraded Super Shuttle in an effort to see off competition from rival British Midland, which had launched its own Diamond Service. Utilising the airline's recently delivered 757-236s, passengers were now offered free drinks and even a hot breakfast on morning flights.

Despite BA's shuttle services being drastically reduced, the 'Shuttle' callsign remains in use today, a reminder of the bygone glory days of UK aviation.

The new airline was a success, becoming the first British carrier to introduce the Embraer ERJ145 in August 1997 and being floated on the London Stock Exchange in June 1998. By this point, BRAL had severed its ties with British Midland to expand its operation with BA. Looking to grow further, BRAL submitted a bid to take over Brymon Airways. BA refused, instead choosing to acquire BRAL and merge it with Brymon Airways to create British Airways CitiExpress. Speaking at the time, BA boss Rod Eddington said that the move was "a significant step forward in building a strong and highly competitive business in the UK regions" to consolidate its short-haul business and reduce fragmentation among its partner airlines.

The new airline commenced operations on March 28, 2002, serving 59 destinations with a varied fleet of 76 aircraft, including 30 ERJ145s, five BAe 146s, 13 ATPs, 13 Jetstream 41s and 15 Bombardier Dash 8-300s.

Initially, the takeover of BRAL heralded a new era for BA Regional. David Evans, the UK

ABOVE: In January 1995, Manx Airlines (Europe) became BA's latest franchise partner, taking over a number of the airline's routes, primarily from its Manchester base

BELOW: To promote the launch of BA Regional in March 1992, several of the 737-236s had *Manchester* titles added to the fuselage to denote their bases, including G-BGDK (c/n 21800) *River Mersey*

general manager, said that growth at the regional subsidiary was set to exceed that of the airline's mainline operation. This was to be achieved through consolidation of its subsidiary carriers and the use of smaller jets to increase frequencies, including nine services out of Manchester, Bristol and Newcastle. Evans said that the regional operation was important for BA, bringing in around £1bn per year.

But a month later, it was announced that 500 jobs would be slashed and 12 routes cut following the Future Size and Shape review, as BA aimed to overhaul its entire operation and return to profitability. The move was designed to reduce its capacity in the UK regions by 8% and deliver annual savings of £20m by 2004. Cardiff was the hardest hit by the move, losing flights to Dublin, Edinburgh, Glasgow and Newcastle. Other services, including Bristol to Brussels and Cork, Plymouth to Cork and Dublin, Southampton to Frankfurt, Jersey to Paris, Newcastle to Cork and Belfast to Sheffield were also slashed.

British Airways' regional operations at Birmingham and Manchester were also brought under the CitiExpress grouping. This saw BAR's fleet of 21 A319s redeployed to London, replaced by 16 ex-CityFlyer Express Avro RJ100s previously based at Gatwick. Following the reorganisation, capacity at Birmingham was cut by around 9%, while at Manchester it remained around the same as before.

In December 2002, further cuts were announced, which involved the removal of CitiExpress's entire turboprop fleet to accelerate its plan to move to an all-jet service by 2005. Humberside-based Eastern Airways would acquire 12 Jetstream 41s. Meanwhile, Loganair would take some of the ATPs, while start-up Air Southwest

ABOVE: BA Connect was the final chapter of the story of British Airways in the regions. Its history was shortlived, with Flybe taking over the subsidiary in March 2007

BELOW: Brymon Airways was rebranded as British Airways Express following its de-merger from Birmingham European Airways. This brought BA's Landor livery back to several regional airports, including Plymouth, where this De Havilland Canada DHC-7 was pictured

acquired three Dash 8-300s, taking over the flag carrier's routes from Plymouth on October 25, 2003, the day after BA pulled out.

Final roll of the dice

Despite high hopes, CitiExpress failed to turn around BA's regional fortunes, suffering annual losses of around £30m due to challenges integrating BAR, BRAL, Manx and Brymon's operations. In August 2005, six flights were cut from its Manchester base to Nice, Cork, Pisa, Rome, Stuttgart and Venice. Willie Walsh, who had become the new CEO of BA in October 2005, went on to call the regional subsidiary "a financial challenge"

In January 2006, it was announced that CitiExpress would be rebranded as BA Connect, a new low-cost carrier for the UK regions. Fifty aircraft would be transferred across, while bases at Birmingham, Manchester, Bristol, Edinburgh, London/City and Southampton would be »

retained. The new division was given a two-year deadline by its parent company to turn a profit or face being shut down.

In a bid to compete with low-cost carriers that had encroached on BA's regional market, BA Connect would see significant changes to the onboard product. Club Europe business class would be removed from the fleet, moving to a single-class product, with fares cut by 40%. Free onboard catering would be swapped for a buy-on-board selection.

However, after losing a further £6m in the first half of 2006, it was announced in November of that year that BA Connect would be sold to regional rival, Flybe. As part of the £150m deal, BA would take a 15% stake in the Exeter-based carrier, but BA Connect services from

ABOVE: British Airways CitiExpress was formed on March 28, 2002, following the merger of BRAL and Brymon Airways

BELOW: In August 1997, BRAL became the first British airline to introduce the Embraer ERJ145. The airline would go on to operate 22 of the type between 1997 and 2002
AIRTEAMIMAGES.COM/
RICHARD HUNT

London/City and the long-haul flights between Manchester and New York were not included.

At the time, BA Connect employed some 1,900 staff and operated 52 routes from 13 regional airports across the UK, with up to 95% of these being point-to-point services, a market that Walsh said was no longer "a strategic part" of BA's business model. The merger, completed in March 2007, turned Flybe into Europe's largest regional airline overnight.

Sadly, it meant the end of the BA flight code on Birmingham's departure boards after 68 years. The airline's long-haul service between Manchester and JFK limped on until October 2008, when it too was dropped, leaving London/Heathrow as the flag carrier's only destination from Manchester, a base it once called its "second home." **AC**